LEE & GRANT

Classic AFVs No2
Their history and how to model them
By Ken Jones and Peter Chamberlain

Patrick Stephens Ltd
in association with Airfix Products Ltd

First published — 1977

British Library Cataloguing in Publication Data

Jones, Kenneth Matthew
    Lee and Grant. — (Classic AFVs; no. 2).
    1. Tanks (Military science) — Models
    I. Title II. Chamberlain, Peter III. Series
    623.74'74   UG446.5

ISBN 0 85059 269 0

Other PSL 'Classics' for modellers

Classic AFVs
No 1 Crusader
by John Milsom, John Sandars and Gerald Scarborough

Classic Aircraft
No 1 Spitfire
by Roy Cross and Gerald Scarborough

No 2 Messerschmitt Bf 109
by Roy Cross and Gerald Scarborough in collaboration with Hans J. Ebert

No 3 P-51 Mustang
by Roy Cross and Gerald Scarborough in collaboration with Bruce Robertson

No 4 Hawker Hurricane
by Bruce Robertson and Gerald Scarborough. Edited by Roy Cross

No 5 Ju 87 Stuka
by Bruce Robertson and Gerald Scarborough

Classic Ships
No 1 HMS Victory
by Noel Hackney
No 2 Mayflower
by Noel Hackney
No 3 Cutty Sark
by Noel Hackney

Text set in 9 on 10 pt Baskerville Medium by Blackfriars Press Limited, Leicester. Printed in Great Britain on Fineblade Art 100 gsm and bound by The Garden City Press, Letchworth. Published by Patrick Stephens Limited, Bar Hill, Cambridge, CB3 8EL, in association with Airfix Products Limited, London SW18.

Contents

Introduction

This is the second volume in a new series of books on classic armoured fighting vehicles (AFVs) centred around the growing range of 1:32 scale model construction kits manufactured by Airfix Products Limited. As with the previous volume on the Crusader, each book in the series will begin by describing the development and fighting record of the particular AFV concerned, then go on to give step-by-step instructions for military modellers wishing to add even more detail to, or convert, the Airfix kits.

Despite being a rushed, interim, design the M3 Medium which forms the subject of this book was a highly successful tank which managed to bloody the nose of the Axis powers in North Africa before the arrival of its successor, the M4 Sherman; and which soldiered on in various guises until the end of the war.

Developed from the American M2 Medium, which never saw action, the M3 was a large and well-armed tank, more sophisticated in many ways than contemporary British, German or Russian designs, and well-liked by its crews despite a high silhouette which made it an easy target. British experience in the desert had shown the need for a larger gun than their existing 2 pdrs, so the M2 was redesigned to take a 75 mm weapon in a sponson on the side of the hull, in addition to the 37 mm gun in its turret. The versatile 75 mm gun was gyro-stabilised so that it *could* be fired on the move, and was also capable of firing high explosive ammunition in addition to armour piercing shells, an attribute lacking in British tank guns. This facility enabled the M3 crews to engage even the dreaded German '88' on more even terms than hitherto.

A British purchasing commission ordered large numbers of M3s in June 1940, but requested alterations to the turret in order to accommodate a British radio. This version, which first saw action at Gazala in 1942, was known to the British as the 'Grant' while its unmodified counterpart was called the 'Lee'.

Production of the M3 ended in December 1942, by which time over 6,000 had been built, and although it was superseded by the Sherman it soldiered on to the end of the war in the Far East and was modified into a number of special-purpose variants — including the famous 'Priest' self-propelled gun — which did see action in Italy and NW Europe.

The M3 carried a crew of six men, had a top speed of 26 mph and armour thickness of up to 57 mm. With a range of 120 miles, and carrying 46 to 65 rounds for its 75 mm gun, it was a useful weapon which played a major role in halting the Afrika Korps and, although often neglected by both historians and modellers, deservedly earned for itself a niche in the history of weapons which won the war as well as a place in any military model collection.

In Part One of this book, Ken Jones describes in detail the development history of the M3 and its fighting record, and includes extensive data tables, diagrams and colour scheme drawings, supported by the numerous clear and fascinating photographs from Peter Chamberlain's extensive collection. In Part Two he then goes on to show how the Airfix 1:32 scale models of the Lee and Grant can be super-detailed and 'customised' to individual taste, and even converted into special-purpose variants such as the CDL, ARV and Priest. This book is thus a veritable mine of information for every military historian, tank and AFV enthusiast and military modeller.

BRUCE QUARRIE

PART ONE
Chapter One

The development of the M3 Medium tank

At the end of World War 1, the United States of America disbanded her tank corps, subordinating a large proportion of the tanks she had retained to the infantry, to be used in a support rôle. The European war had left the country with over 30 million dollars tied up in tanks, yet it would be another 20 years or so before the United States would be forced into building tanks on a large scale and to gain a predominance in production of tanks which, at the time, could only be imagined.

The first year of the 1920s saw General Rockenback attempting to retain or reform the tank corps as an indigenous arm, though he was defeated along with such far-seeing men as Majors George Patton, Sereno Brett and Dwight Eisenhower, who were at the only United States Tank School. An act of Congress was passed rejecting all ideas of a separate tank corps; the tanks would go to the infantry and would be their sole responsibility.

Some steps were taken to get the thoughts and requirements, should the need arise, of serving officers on the type of tanks that would be needed. A staff major, who had served on the Anglo-American Tank Commission in the previous war, R. E. Carlson, wrote a paper on the development of the tank which laid down the possible requirements for light and medium tanks in a future United States Tank Corps. The aftermath of war affected the country, just as it did her allies, and in such a climate of mass demobilisation, unemployment and restricted government spending, it is not surprising that Carlson's paper went largely unnoticed and unread. Two years or so later the General Staff put out a directive on the United States' future armour requirements. Drawing heavily on Carlson's work, they used his guidelines of light tanks, machine-gun armed, of five tons, and mediums weighing up to 20 tons with machine-gun and cannon armament. The directives did not hold much water with a lot of American generals and so the United States really only 'flirted' with the ideas of tanks. Well known personalities claimed that the tank was only a means to an end, ensuring that the infantryman could reach his objective and all future machines, should they materialise, should be designed with this aim in sight. The thinking followed the infantry support course, memories were short, as always, the ideas of an armoured thrust were disregarded, the cavalry would retain their horses and not re-equip with tanks. It appeared that the decimation of cavalry by machine-guns, albeit static machine-guns, in World War 1 was wrongly documented and had never really happened.

Despite her cautious approach to tank design and production, the United States began to build tanks, piecemeal, at the national arsenal at Rock Island, Illinois, in the artillery plant. The two 'new' designs that appeared in 1921 and 1922 were both mediums. The second tank, an improved version of the first, was similar to the British Medium D, and had a rotating turret which mounted a 57 mm gun. The Medium Tank TI followed from Rock Island in 1926; weighing 23 tons, it was well over the estimated 15-ton engineers' bridging and transportation limits. This vehicle was later improved, re-engined, uprating its horse power by 138 and was designated T1E1. When, two years later, the United States assembled its whole mechanised force at Fort Meade, Maryland, it still consisted mainly of World War 1 heavies and Renault light tanks.

The T2 made its debut in 1930. Weighing 15 tons with a 312 hp Liberty engine, it closely resembled contemporary Vickers designs. The same year a mixed mechanised force was raised at Fort Eustis in Virginia, consisting of armoured cars, cavalry and mechanised artillery. All the experimental tanks were made available to this force to supplement deficiencies and the old World War 1 tanks. The resultant

Medium Tank T5E2. Experimental self-propelled carriage for 75 mm Pack Howitzer. Note rangefinder in small turret on hull top.

Medium Tank M2. This vehicle carried four .30 cal sponson mounts in addition to other armaments.

course was favourable, the cavalry took over the mobile force development from the infantry and set up its centre at Fort Knox, Kentucky, though as usual, very little progress was made.

At about this time the so-called 'eccentric', Walter Christie, who had submitted earlier designs, introduced his wheel-cum-track light tank, the sleek appearance of which made all other 'traditional' designs seem rather old-fashioned. Christie demonstrated his vehicle to the army who ordered, with their usual prudence, five vehicles. The story of Walter Christie's arguments with the United States Defence Department, and the adaptation of his ideas by the Soviets and British are legend, and have no place here; suffice to say, once again, the Americans ignored what other countries grasped as a revolutionary idea. The American Army plodded on buying small numbers of tanks to Christie's design and adopting the fashionable light fast tanks, which evolved from contemporaneous designs and were built at Rock Island, culminating in the progenitor of the Lee and Grant mediums, the M2.

The M2 medium tank designed at Rock Island was developed from the various stages of T5 mediums, which went through three phases until standardised as the medium tank M2 in 1939. Orders were placed for this vehicle, traditionally small ones initially, of course, as befitted United States thinking of the 1920s and '30s, though events were shaping in Europe at this time which would shatter all American rumination on tank development. At dawn on September 1

1939, two army groups of the German Wehrmacht, supported by the Luftwaffe, swept into Poland. A new word was coined, 'Blitzkrieg'; the Poles, unable to contain the armoured thrusts, were defeated in 18 days. The world would be at war again, although the Americans were determined not to be drawn into this new European conflict as they had been in 1917. However, as the war progressed to the British withdrawal at Dunkirk, the Americans knew they would have to make some preparations, albeit maintaining a low profile, and improve their armoured forces. It was blatantly obvious that America was severely lacking in any positive armoured strength. She found herself in a position similar to her entry into World War 1 with a paucity of what was then the dominant battlefield weapon, the machine-gun; now events had turned full circle, the tank was the dominant weapon and American forces had very few tanks to go around.

The M2 medium, and its improved successor the M2A1, looked — and were — outmoded and outgunned in the light of events from Europe, since they were designed to specifications over 15 years old. Although ordnance had requested larger calibre weapons, the M2 fielded a 37 mm tank gun which was, in retrospect, equal to co-existent German guns of the Panzer force. In July 1940 General George Marshall, Chief of General Staff, told General Adna R. Chaffee to take over all armoured forces from the infantry and cavalry and form two armoured divisions which would have support battalions; to re-equip these forces 1,000 M2A1s were to be ordered and would be produced solely for the new tank corps at the rate of ten per day. This figure was a little optimistic for the time if only Rock Island was to be

Lee & Grant

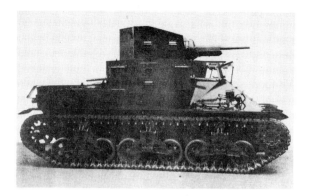

Right Medium Tank M2A1. Improved version of the Medium Tank M2, with new turret and increased armour. **Below right** *Medium Tank M3 wooden mock-up.*

the sole producer, although plans had been formulated the previous month to this end. The National Munitions Programme was passed on June 30 1940, and by July 10 General Chaffee had formed his new armoured force. All he needed was the tanks to go with it.

On June 9 1940, Lieutenant General William Knudsen, formerly of General Motors Corporation and now Chief of the National Defence Programme, approached Mr K. T. Keller, President of the powerful Chrysler Corporation, with a view to Chrysler's production lines at Detroit turning out the new M2A1 medium tank. Ordnance had assumed that large concerns such as the American Locomotive Company and Baldwins could, if the need ever did arise, easily switch to tank production because of the nature of their industries. As the Rock Island Arsenal was building two pilot models of the M2A1, General Wesson, Chief of Ordnance, allowed Chrysler engineers to study the vehicle; it was envisaged that 1,741 of these vehicles could be produced in 18 months. Chrysler were given 4½ weeks to estimate the switching of plant, buildings and equipment to tank production, and came up with the idea of a self-contained tank arsenal geared to full-scale output of tanks. Surprisingly, they were given the go-ahead on this 21 million dollar project; Mr Keller assuring General Wesson that Chrysler could produce tanks whilst the arsenal was being built around them. On July 17 1940 Chrysler estimates were complete: the M2A1 would cost $33,500, a fixed price on which the ordnance committee prudently affixed an escalator clause. The following month, on August 15, the formal contracts were signed. The 1,000 M2A1s had to be delivered by August 1942 and the tank arsenal to produce them had to be completed by September 1941, dates which Chrysler proved to be over-ample in time, once they entered production with the later Grants and Lees.

Chrysler produced a wooden mock-up of M2A1 once they were in possession of a full set of drawings from Rock Island to work out plant required and machine tool costings for mass production of the vehicles in the proposed arsenal. Then, as a result of General Chaffee's discussions with the Ordnance Department Committee at Aberdeen, considering the feasibility of mounting a 75 mm gun in the M2A1 (which had been tried already as the T5E2 project) the M2A1 concept was cancelled in favour of the then 'undesigned' M3 project. The ordnance design committee calculated this would take three months to materialise. August 28 1940 saw the cancellation of the original order for 1,000 M2A1s placed with

Right and above right *Close-up and rear view of M2 Medium Tank with British-designed turret for M3.*

The development of the M3 Medium tank

7

Above *Medium Tank M3 pilot model under test.* Below *Rear view of pilot model.*

Chrysler, who were starting to tool up; and Elmer Dodt, a Chrysler engineer, left for Aberdeen to advise the design team on the application of mass-production techniques to the new M3 design.

The M3 design allowed for the main armament, a 75 mm gun, to be mounted in a sponson in the hull front. A cast, fully rotating turret, mounting a 37 mm gun was fitted on top. At this time the idea of a 75 mm gun in a 360 degree rotating turret was not viable although, running concurrently in design, another tank — the M4, later named General Sherman — was in its early state. This branded the M3 from the outset

as a classic stop-gap weapon; a tank which would have to make do until ordnance could hurry through the M4.

A tank commission — part of a general purchasing commission — from Britain had arrived in the United States, looking for suitable American designs to replenish the sadly depleted British armoured force; the majority of British armour had been lost in France, and the commission was buying up — for cash! — enterprising American designs. They settled for the M3 and suggested a re-designed lower turret to house radio equipment in accordance with standard British practice, plus many other small design suggestions. It was decided to produce both versions of the M3 simultaneously, since the British would take a share of the American-designed turret version as well. The British called their modified type the General Grant and the American version General Lee, after the two famous American Civil War personalities.

Design of the M3 was only 90 per cent settled by December 1940, and ordnance gave themselves until the last day of January in the new year to finalise matters. Chrysler were forging ahead with the tank arsenal at Detroit in anticipation of receiving the last drawings and the go-ahead on the M3.

Work had started on Chrysler's arsenal on September 9 1940, on a 113-acre site outside Detroit at Warren Township; the government footed the bill for the land and plant equipment for the building itself, which covered a floor area of nearly 77,000 square yards. Work was completed by the end of January 1941, as Chrysler engineers, along with those from Baldwin and American Loco, finalised produc-

Lee & Grant

tion techniques. All was now set for production. Other firms such as Pullman-Standard Car Company, Pressed Steel and Lima Locomotive were later brought in with a host of small subcontractors to produce the stop-gap design. In addition to Chrysler's orders, American Locomotive received an order for 685 M3s and Baldwin 534 vehicles. The pilot models rolled out in April 1941, American Loco and Baldwin's first, then Chrysler's on Good Friday, the 11th of the month. This Chrysler pilot model was presented by Chrysler subscriptions to the Government as a gift. Chrysler sent an M3 to Aberdeen for testing on May 3, keeping another tank back as a pattern for the detail changes the ordnance board were bound to suggest.

The production lines went into top gear from July 8 1941 onwards. The Lease-Lend Act had been passed by Congress on March 8 the same year, so output was pushed up, and all the stops were pulled out for tank production to Britain and the USSR in addition to home needs. By July 10 1942 Chrysler alone had produced 3,100 M3 tanks, and the oft-forgotten

Right and below *M3 Medium Tanks on the assembly line in Chrysler's Detroit Arsenal.*

Medium Tank M3.

Canadian subsidiary at Montreal Locomotive Works had produced 1,157 M3s for the Canadian Army. A month later production of M3s ceased in favour of the M4 Sherman.

The M3, the classic stop-gap design — production-wise — was dead! The lines in the tank arsenals switched to the M4 virtually without any interruption in schedules. The M3 had been in production from July 8 1941 until August 3 1942, just over one year. Supplies of this tank to the British had given them breathing space and proved to be a large contributing factor to the turn of events in North Africa, the theatre in which the M3 made its debut and saw its first action.

Chapter Two

The Lee and Grant in detail

The basic M3 design was very simple; the fighting compartment was roomy, the turret adequate, but the vehicle was too high. The height of the tank was dictated by the need to lead the transmission from the centre of a radial engine to the gearbox at the front, under the turret basket.

The driver sat to the left and front of the fighting compartment. Directly below his vision port was the instrument panel with speedometer — with integral odometer — rev counter, ammeter, voltmeter, oil pressure, temperature gauges and a clock. The gear change, (clutch) brake and accelerator pedals were conventionally laid out as were the two steering levers. The transmission housing was to the driver's right; the handbrake was mounted on to the rear of the bell housing. If the .30 calibre Brownings were fitted in the bow embrasures, the driver could fire

The Chrysler prototype Medium Tank M3 showing the twin bow machine-guns.

these. In the Lee the radio set was to the driver's left, about shoulder level. It was mounted in the turret on the Grant in accordance with British practice.

The 75 mm gunner sat behind and to the right of the driver, and his loader stood behind to the left rear side of the breech. Down the centre of the vehicle, through the fighting compartment, ran the propeller shaft and clutch linkage encased for crew protection and safety. The turret was offset to the left-hand side and the turret basket took up the bulk of the space in the fighting compartment, though the M3 was still one of the roomiest tanks in service in any army.

The traverse — hydraulic or hand — was controlled by the 37 mm gunner who, along with his loader and commander, traversed with the turret basket as a complete unit. Their adjustable seats were fixed to the turret cage sides. The turret gunner sat to the left of the gun, with his loader to the right. The tank commander sat behind them to the left in both Grant and Lee turrets. In the Lee he was provided with a sepa-

Above Early production of the Medium Tank M3 with British-designed turret. Below Interior of the Lee in British service showing wireless set.

rate rotating cupola fitted with a .30 cal Browning machine-gun. The Grant had a circular hatch with a split hinged cover with a single periscope for the commander's use. The No 19 radio set was mounted in the turret 'bustle' behind the commander, which could be worked by him or the loader. This turret also had a 2-inch bomb thrower on the right front and two protectoscopes in revolver ports. A .30 cal Browning machine-gun could be mounted on to a pintle fitted to the cupola ring of the commander's hatchway.

The Lee machine-gun cupola had three protecto-scopes for the commander's use, and most of this small turret was taken up by the breech of the Browning machine-gun, the rest by the commander's head when he was fighting the tank. When Lees were used in British service this gun was usually removed, or, as in Burma, the whole cupola was sometimes removed and a plain hatchway substituted as found on the Grant. Both turrets shared a common gun mounting for the 37 mm gun and .30 cal co-axial machine-gun. Ammunition stowage for the 37 mm gun was provided for ready use inside the walls of the turret basket and along the rear wall of the fighting compartment. The 75 mm rounds were dispersed about the fighting compartment clear of the rotating turret basket.

The fighting compartment was fitted with an entry door either side, each of which contained a protectoscope mounted in a revolver port, which hinged upwards for ventilation and to allow a pistol to be fired from it. Later models had these omitted or the doors were retrospectively welded up. The auxiliary generator, which provided a power source for the tank systems, such as the gun turret traverse, was mounted on the engine compartment bulkhead.

The engine compartment varied, slightly, in its precise layout according to the power plant fitted, but always contained the fuel tanks either side of the engine, access to which was through rear hull doors. An engine change meant the removal of the rear armoured decking though most maintenance could be carried out to Wright-engined tanks from the rear access hatches.

The first M3s had Curtiss Wright-designed R975 9-cylinder radial aero-engines, petrol ignition, which were adapted for tank use as the Continental EC2 or CI. This radial engine was air-cooled with — because it was an aero design — an excellent power to weight ratio; a smaller version was fitted into the M3 light tanks. The engine compartment had to be large to take the Continental radial motor which developed around 353 hp at 2,400 rpm and, without an airstream to cool it, became heavy on oil consumption, though it required minimum maintenance and was reliable. The 'clonking' engine note of this motor was unmistakable. The engine drove the tank via a gearbox with five forward speeds and one reverse, all synchromesh. Power was transmitted by the propeller shaft from the clutch mounted on the front of the engine to the gearbox beside the driver; from the gearbox power was transferred to sprockets and thence to the tracks.

Sequence showing the removal of Grant engines for maintenance. These are 9-cylinder Curtiss Wright R975s.

The Lee and Grant in detail

Above *Medium Tank M3A1 side view.* **Below** *Medium Tank M3A1.*

The M3s were steered by two levers, ostensibly one for each track. This type of steering system was called controlled differential, the gearbox not being used for steering the tank. This system had been developed by the Cleveland Tractor Company and it worked by applying braking power to either sprocket by retarding the driven subsidiary pinion to it. The turning circle was 37 feet as the braking ratios were equal. This system was not really designed for the sharp turns often called for in 'open space' mobile warfare such as the Western Desert.

The Wright Aero-engines later became difficult to obtain during the step-up in M3 production, so a radial diesel, the Guiberson, was fitted. The British received some of these and suffixed the designation M3 (diesel). Another diesel engine that was fitted was a General Motors-designed power plant; this was a liquid-cooled, in-line twin bank, the 6-71 or model 6046, which developed about 375 hp at 2,100 rpm. This engine had a good torque at low speed and was very reliable. The British used the Guiberson diesel models in the Western Desert. A friend of the author still has his notebook, SO book 137, from when he was with HQ 1st Armoured Brigade Group, Tank Reorganisation. An entry dated October 21 1942 lists the movement of two Grant diesels to 10 Corps. These vehicles were T24053 and T24061 and both only had 80 or so miles on the clock. At this time the Sherman was the front-line runner, but the Grants and Lees were still in demand. The logistical difficulties caused by diesel-powered vehicles was obvious, as in common with German tanks, most British vehicles had petrol engines fitted.

Another engine fitted into M3s was the Ford-developed GAA V8 petrol engine; water-cooled, it developed 450 hp at 2,600 rpm. Perhaps the most unusual engine ever fitted though, was the successful Chrysler-built and developed A57 multi-bank 30-cylinder engine which developed 370 hp at 2,400 rpm. This compound engine, which Chrysler engineers developed in a record time of four months, was really five existing Chrysler-designed engines

Above *Grant I.* **Above right** *Medium Tank M3A2.*

working a common crankshaft. The engines were built by Chrysler Jefferson, and were known affectionately by the troops as 'Dionne Quints' or Egg Beaters. They were reliable, economical engines, although they did pose a few problems with maintenance and oil consumption. One version of the M3 line was fitted with the A57, which called for a redesigned engine compartment and lengthening of the hull itself. The suspension consequently had to be re-spaced and the tank was standardised as the M3A4. Chrysler fitted the later Shermans with this engine, though it was first tested in an M3 on November 15 1941 over a 4,000 mile march; the resulting reports were favourable.

The antiquated-looking suspension system used on the M3 series and the later M4 series initial production models was of a type standardised on the early American vehicles, and termed vertical volute suspension. This uncomplicated suspension mounted two rubber-tyred wheels on pivoted arms bearing against a vertical spring, which was protected by an armoured bracket. The whole assembly, which had a return roller mounted on top on the early variants, and to the rear on later ones, was a self-contained unit. It could be bolted or unbolted very easily to the side of the hull, and damaged or unserviceable units could be replaced by another part in field workshops or, if need be, by light aid detachments. This easily maintained suspension gave a 'solid' steady ride, but later gave way to the horizontal volute suspension on later Shermans. All M3s, despite those used for testing new systems, were fitted only with vertical volute suspension. The tracks fitted to M3s were rubber, dry-pinned blocks, and the sprocket teeth bore into these pins, protruding as they did from either side of the track links, transferring motion to the track. Various patterns were tried out on the rubber track pads, and later in the production period some steel tracks were tried on M3s, several of which were so equipped and sent to Russia for use against the Germans there.

With the exception of the M3A1 with a cast hull built by Baldwin and the welded vehicles — very few were built, about a dozen only — the production M3s were riveted. The old arguments about riveted tanks were as common as the diesel fuel versus petrol topic. It was thought by some schools that a hit on a riveted

tank would produce sprung rivets which would spin around the interior of the vehicle cutting the crew to ribbons, just as it was stated that high octane fuel ignited more readily than diesel fuel. Whilst there is certainly a lot of truth in the latter statement, really it was exploding interior-stowed ammunition that was the main cause of tank destruction, and if the M3 was pierced there was an even distribution around the vehicle of ready use ammunition to explode. Except for the 88 mm gun, the M3s could not always be pierced by German anti-tank and tank guns, and the M3 proved it could take punishment. It was found that the hull doors were a weak point, so on later production models these were either entirely omitted in production or later welded up.

Radio and internal communications systems were fitted to all M3 models. The rear turret bustle on the Grant took the British No 19 radio set, while Lees in British service had this transceiver beside the driver, in the place of American equipment. The Number 19 set had two transceivers, the A set which was for long-range work and the B set for short-range. All crew members had a junction box for plugging their headsets into the Tannoy intercommunication system within the tank. American vehicles usually mounted the SCR 508 radio, which had an interphone facility for internal crew communications. The SCR 506 was fitted to command vehicles.

Tank battles are controlled more easily by radio, though disadvantages of the system are many, good clear reception of these vintage World War 2 radio sets being one since VHF communication was not available for tanks at this time. Range was not very good, and although one would think that the open spaces of the desert would improve things, this was not so. The interception of opposing forces' transmissions to gain information on deployments, etc, was practised by both sides as radio silence was hard to enforce, though intelligent use of radio in tanks did bring rewards.

The M3s were fitted with a CO_2 fire fighting system consisting of a fixed 10 lb extinguisher system and a hand-operated 4 lb extinguisher. As in most vehicles little chance of using these occurred in action as a bad hit usually signified a 'bale out'; few tank men would stay entombed in the vehicle to fight a fire with the threat of exploding ammunition. However, for a

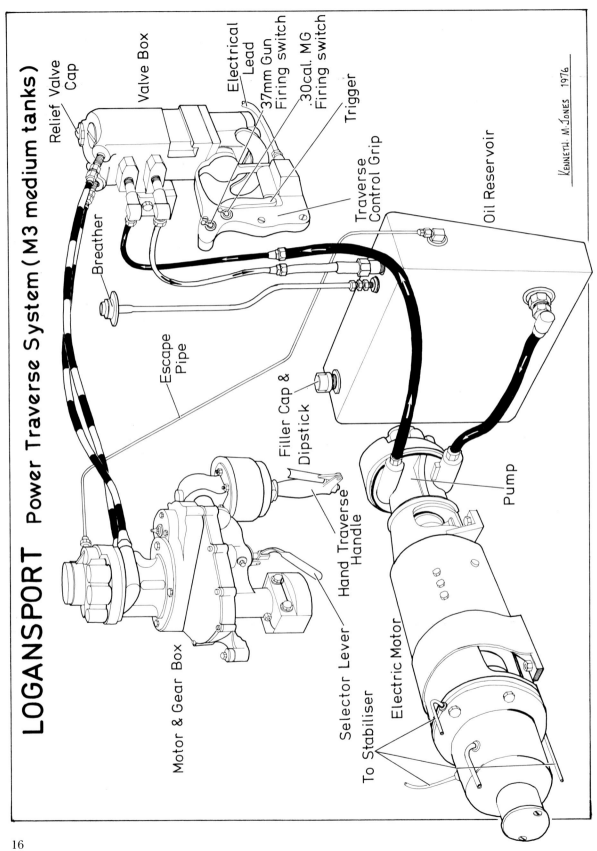

LOGANSPORT Power Traverse System (M3 medium tanks)

Relief Valve Cap

Valve Box

Electrical Lead

37mm Gun Firing switch

.30cal. MG Firing switch

Trigger

Breather

Traverse Control Grip

Oil Reservoir

Escape Pipe

Filler Cap & Dipstick

Hand Traverse Handle

Motor & Gear Box

Selector Lever

To Stabiliser

Electric Motor

Pump

KENNETH. M. JONES 1976

small internal fire, CO_2 extinguishers were non-toxic and fairly safe to use, as any fumes would be vented by the extractor fans.

Powered traverse was fitted to all M3s. This was the Logansport-developed system, which gave a full 360 degree rotation of the turret in about 15 seconds at fast speed. The system worked on hydraulic principles; oil was driven through the system by a pump powered by an electric motor. The powered traverse could be disengaged and the turret traversed by hand if required or in the event of a power systems failure.

Electrical power for the traverse mechanism was provided by the two 12-volt batteries incorporated into the vehicle's electrical system, though powered traverse was only advised with the tank engine or auxiliary generator working to prevent a drain on these. Electrical current was transferred from the vehicle's hull earth return, via a turret collector ring, thence to the 1¼ hp electric motor encased in its mounting on the turret floor. The electric motor shared a common mounting with the system's oil pump, supplied by oil from an oil reservoir tank bolted to the wall of the turret basket near the gunner's feet. The reservoir held 2.2 gallons of oil to charge the system and was fitted with a breather valve to allow for oil expansion and to allow air to escape from the system. The electric motor and pump assembly worked both the turret traverse and gun stabiliser mechanisms.

The gunner's traverse controls consisted of two separate units; his left hand worked the manual traversing handle, system selector lever on the motor and gearbox mounting fixed to the turret ring, and his right hand worked the spade grip for powered traverse also attached to the turret ring. The diagram clearly shows these features and components. The motor and gearbox, which was provided with a reversible gear, was driven by oil pressure discharged to either of its two valves by the spade grip control, transmitting power to a pinion, via the gear train, to the toothed gear around the turret ring. The selector lever for power or manual traverse was incorporated in this unit as was the geared handle for traversing the turret manually.

The power traverse control consisted of a movable spade grip operating handle, fitted to a valve box which was attached to the turret ring. The firing switches for the 37 mm gun and .30 calibre machine-gun were mounted on this grip. By squeezing a grip or trigger switch the spade grip was unlocked from its central or neutral position and could be turned on its axis in the required direction of turret rotation. The spade grip; releasing the trigger locked the turret on the opening and closing of which determined the direction of travel. A third valve, the relief valve, was incorporated into the equipment to control the oil pressure of the whole system. Slight movement of the spade grip in either direction provided a slow traverse, pushing the handle right across against its stops produced top speed traverse which effected full rotation in 15 seconds. The turret came to a dead stop at the required degree of traverse by centralising the spade grip; releasing the trigger locked the turret on the selected bearing. The whole system was activated by a master switch contained in a fused circuit box mounted to the gunner's left side.

The Logansport traverse system was simple, and gave very little trouble. It was self-lubricating and needed the minimum of maintenance, depending as it did upon the circulation of oil for its operation. The direction of flow was determined by the direction in which the gunner moved his spade grip control. When the system was switched on by the gunner, with the tank engine running, oil would be forced through a pressure pipe to the valve box from the reservoir, activating the relief valve on the valve box allowing the passage of oil from the valve box through the return pipe to the reservoir. This can be determined from study of the diagram. Pressure built up in the system almost instantaneously; with his left hand the gunner would push the selector lever up to engage power traverse and rotate the spade grip with his right hand to the required bearing. This opened one of the two valves in the valve box, closed the other and allowed oil to pass to the motor on the turret gearbox, again the side of which was determined by the direction of traverse selected. Oil flow through the motor pump operated the attached gear train and rotated the turret, opposite movement of the spade grip reversed the whole system. Excess oil was allowed to escape from the pump via a pipe fitted between the motor and the oil reservoir, keeping the hydraulic pressure constant.

Gyro stabilisers were not new to gunnery systems, neither were they wholly successful in operation, but the M3 was the first tank to have a mass-produced system fitted, developed and built by the Westinghouse Company. It was fitted to most production models in the M3 series. As two types of gun were carried, either the M2 or M3 (the latter having the longer barrel of the two), later production models were set up to one common setting on the stabiliser, that of the longer barrel and increased weight of the M3 version. This is why the prominent muzzle coun-

Medium Tank M3A3 with counter-weight on the M2 75 mm gun.

WESTINGHOUSE GYRO STABILISER SYSTEM M3 MEDIUMS

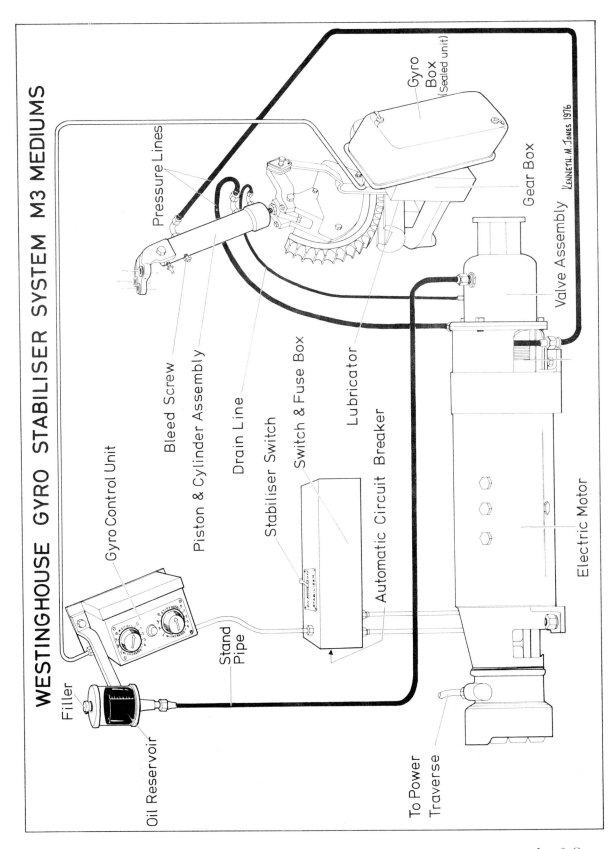

Pressure Lines

Gyro Box (Sealed unit)

Gear Box

Kenneth M. Jones 1976

Valve Assembly

Bleed Screw

Piston & Cylinder Assembly

Drain Line

Stabiliser Switch

Switch & Fuse Box

Lubricator

Automatic Circuit Breaker

Electric Motor

Gyro Control Unit

Filler

Oil Reservoir

Stand Pipe

To Power Traverse

Medium Tank M3A4 with side doors eliminated and an M3 75 mm gun.

terweight is seen on some M2 guns to compensate for the loss in barrel weight when fitted in a tank with a gyro stabiliser set up for the later M3 gun.

The Westinghouse stabiliser system worked by an electrically controlled hydraulic system and was expected to control the gun's movements in elevation only, within a maximum vertical angle of plus or minus 20 minutes if the gun trunnions oscillated through an angle of plus or minus 2.5 degrees. The intention of the stabilisers, when they were fitted to turret and hull main armament, was to reduce the effect of oscillation of the guns if the vehicle moved over uneven ground. The ultimate aim was to perfectly balance the gun — which was easier said than done in a tank — by reducing the friction of the gun trunnions to almost zero, keeping the gun balanced, and relying upon the inertia of the weapon to keep it fixed upon any set angle regardless of the vehicle's movements. The stabiliser would hold the gun on any predetermined angle to the earth's surface, but any change of direction or terrain such as depressions or gradients could not be coped with as the gun stabiliser would only keep the gun to the angle set and was only really suited to flatter terrain, such as the desert, having been adapted from the same principles applied to stabilisers employed on ship armament. This is perhaps one reason why some crews did not switch in the stabiliser, either they did not have time or could not be bothered with testing or setting it up. Besides,

in its early form the Westinghouse stabiliser was not completely successful.

It was recommended that it should only be used when firing from a moving tank, and that driving at a constant speed with smooth gear changes and no sudden turns. This was fine for neatly arranged peacetime manoeuvres and the like, but British tank drivers were taught to weave about, slow down and speed up in combat to make their vehicles more difficult targets, so one can imagine the stabiliser being 'confused' under these circumstances. The gunner had to make corrections with his handwheel whilst the stabiliser was operative to compensate for the terrain or shift of target, though if he turned his gun

Medium Tank M3A5. Note welded side door.

through full elevation or depression with the stabiliser engaged he could overload the tank battery circuit and ruin the gyroscopic control unit. This circuit was protected by a circuit-breaker but if the system was overloaded it took over a minute to re-engage. A minute is a long time in a tank-to-tank battle for a gunner to spend 'fiddling' with electrical equipment when he should be laying and firing his gun, so some gunners ignored the system whilst others used it, despite the fact that the prime objective of the stabiliser was to minimise re-laying. It takes a large stretch of the imagination to picture gunners using the stabiliser in action where speed counted in laying and firing, though for long range engagements over smoother terrain, for example in artillery-type bombardments using high explosive against soft-skin vehicles or the like, with time to choose targets, the system merited itself.

The system for both guns was powered by a 1¼ hp electric motor. For the turret gun the motor powered both the stabiliser and traverse systems and was mounted on the turret floor. The hull gun had the electric motor along with the remainder of the stabiliser unit fitted to the side of the gun mounting.

The stabiliser used hydraulic oil which was contained in a glass reservoir of two pints capacity, mounted at the highest point possible in the system. The oil was gravity-fed to the hydraulic pump, driven by the electric motor, which pumped the oil under pressure via two lines to the hydraulic cylinder unit, one end of which was fixed to the gun mounting and the piston to the moving gun via the gearbox. The

US Army Medium Tanks M3, late production, on manoeuvres in England.

two oil pressure pipes ran to the cylinder, one above the piston and one below, so varying pressure via these lines operated the piston. Equal pressure from both stabilised the gun. Excess oil was allowed to drain from the pressurised cylinder by a drain pipe fitted to the bottom of the piston housing.

The flow of oil to the piston was determined by the valve control unit in front of the pump which had one driving and two driven pinions, powered from the electric motor. The oil pressure in the lines to the cylinder was controlled by a rocker switch, which received its impulses electro-magnetically from the gyroscopes and transmitted mechanical power to either of two needle valves contained in its assembly. This rocker valve made either valve open or close and maintained a directly proportionate feed of oil between the two along the supply pressure lines to the cylinder.

The two electromagnetic switches that operated the rocker switch, which in turn controlled the needle valves, were fed with varying electric current from two small gyroscopic motors contained within a sealed unit. This unit was adjusted and controlled from the gyro control box passing information for stiffness and recoil via the hydraulic system to the gun. The gyro-motors inside the box ran at about 14,000 rpm and any movement of the vehicle caused the gyroscopes to react by varying the current via each electromagnetic switch to the rocker switch controlling the hydraulics. If the vehicle was stable the gyros passed equal current to the electromagnets which centralised the rocker switch, which in turn closed both needle valves. This maintained an equal pressure in the circuit which centralised the piston and thence stabilised the gun. Any deviation from this was 'sensed' by the gyros transmitted via the unit to the gun, bearing in mind that a pressure variation in one pipe was automatically compensated for in the other.

When the gun fired with the stabiliser engaged, allowance was made in the system to keep the gun in balance as it recoiled. A switch in the circuit was activated by the recoiling gun; the switch was mounted on the gun cradle and allowed a greater surge of current to operate one electromagnetic switch, closing an oil pressure valve exerting extra pressure to the stabilising piston, not forgetting that the open valve would compensate its pipeline and equalise the increased pressure imparted from the other valve, thus keeping the gun in balance. As the gun ran out after firing, the recoil switch closed the circuit and returned the gun under normal stabiliser control.

Setting up the stabiliser system initially was largely a hit or miss procedure for the gunner. Time was obviously needed to pre-set the equipment if the gunner used the system. The gunner could not set it up in action, he had to set it up during a halt or a lull in the fighting, so that it could be turned on at a moment's notice at the switchbox. The gunner had two control boxes in addition to the gyro unit; one, the master switchbox, fused with an automatic circuit breaker, and a control box with recoil and stiffness

Lee & Grant

controls, consisting of variable resistors with a red system activation light.

With the tank engine or auxiliary generator running, the gunner would ensure that sufficient oil was contained in his reservoir to work the system and check for leaks. He would then have to disengage the elevating rack from the worm wheel on his manual-elevation gear to enable the stabiliser to operate. He turned the sealed gyro unit by hand to its vertical position; this was connected to the gearbox by a friction clutch to keep it in place in relation to the gun's horizontal axis.

Next the stiffness control on the control unit was set initially to position number 5 and the system switched on and allowed a two minutes warm-up period. The gunner then thumped the gun breech with his hand and if the gun oscillated he would reduce the stiffness control until oscillation ceased. By reducing his control he was varying the resistance in the circuit to so reduce the current fed to the system. The system often needed readjusting in action if it was used because temperature changes would alter the oil pressure in the system caused by changing oil viscosity.

As with stiffness, the gunner also set his recoil control to 5 initially, layed his gun horizontally and fired a round with the vehicle stationary. Again, it was difficult to set the recoil when in action, or to fire off rounds at nothing in particular while halted. When the gun recoiled the gunner had to look to see if the breech depressed on firing, if it did he increased his control, while if the breech elevated itself on firing he reduced current to the system. Re-adjustment was

British gunner loading the M3 75 mm gun in a Grant.

trial and error during firing until harmony was obtained. Theoretically the operation of stabilised guns in tanks is sound, but to make it work in practice is another story. Again, theoretically, American tanks had a tactical advantage with stabilised guns, which purported to reduce the time the gunner spent laying his gun in elevation to a bare minimum. Stabilisers were not fitted to British or German-produced tanks during World War 2, though since then matters have come a long way and improved vastly. Since 1948 British tanks have used a much refined gun stabiliser, far more effective in operation than the early Westinghouse equipment that was fitted to the M3 mediums.

Unit of the Canadian Armoured Division, Fort Garry Horse, on exercises with M3 Medium Tanks.

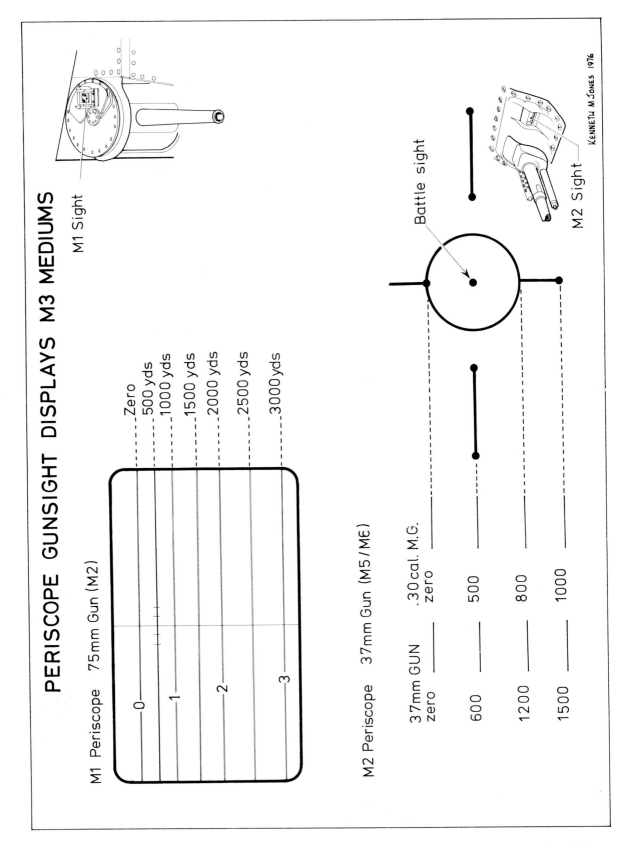

PERISCOPE GUNSIGHT DISPLAYS M3 MEDIUMS

M1 Sight

M1 Periscope 75mm Gun (M2)

Zero
500 yds
1000 yds
1500 yds
2000 yds
2500 yds
3000 yds

0
1
2
3

M2 Periscope 37mm Gun (M5/M6)

Battle sight

M2 Sight

KENNETH M JONES 1976

37mm GUN
zero

600

1200

1500

.30 cal. M.G.
zero

500

800

1000

The sponson-mounted 75 mm gun was layed on target by the M1 periscope which was fitted with a telescopic sight. The armoured top cover of the periscope can be seen over the sponson gun mounting in the photographs and drawings. The periscope was linked to the gun mounting and moved along its sector plate as the gun traversed, also transporting the gunner on his seat.

The periscope contained two parallel mirrors inclined at 45 degrees and protected by armoured glass blocks. A telescopic gunsight was mounted vertically between the mirrors, projecting the range scale to the bottom mirror and thence to the gunner's field of view. The telescope had an adjustable vertical graticule and fixed horizontal ones, representing ranges from 0 to 3,000 yards in early models, and up to 3,500 in later sights fitted to vehicles with the M3 gun. Between the 0 and 1,000 yards graticule a 500 yards line was provided with vertical graduations to the horizontal scale to aid the gunner in aiming-off on deflection shots. The function of these marks was similar to radial rings on an anti-aircraft ring gunsight when used on deflection shooting.

The telescope was provided with a simple circuit powered by a battery to illuminate the range scales, which could be adjusted vertically and horizontally by two adjusting wheels on the rear of the periscope mounting. The periscope was fitted with a padded eyepiece or 'brow pad' for ease of operation when the vehicle was moving. The diagram shows the periscope gunsight display clearly.

The 37 mm gun telescope was contained within a similar periscope to the M1 fitted on the 75 mm gun, although it gave a different aiming display. The sight performed a dual function in that it sighted the co-axial .30 calibre machine-gun on the same graticules as the 37 mm gun, only the ranges differed: 0 to 1,500 for the 37 mm gun and 0 to 1,000 yards for the machine-gun. The sight display was a circle with a centre spot which acted as the battle sight for both guns. Deflection shooting was provided for by graduations on the horizontal axis. Again the diagram shows the display which the turret gunner saw through his periscope.

Two versions of the 75 mm gun were fitted to the M3 medium tanks, the M2 and the M3, the latter being the longer of the two, 118.375 inches against 91.75 inches. The basic M2 gun was designed by ordnance at Westervliet Arsenal, being adapted from the French 75 mm field gun which the United States had adopted as standard at the end of World War 1. Initial orders were placed by the government for 1,308 guns and mountings for the M3 tank in which it would be fitted. These were ordered straight off the drawing board, whilst the tank was also in the design stage, in fact both were produced and developed concurrently. The first guns produced were built in time to be fitted to the M3 pilot models.

The 75 mm gun was a dual-purpose and semi-automatic gun. This is to say that it could fire armour-piercing and high explosive rounds (in addi-

Close-up of Lee turret showing British smoke dischargers.

tion to other miscellania, such as smoke shells) expressly designed for it, and that ejection and recocking were carried out by mechanical means when the gun recoiled and ran out. Loading after the first shot also featured automatic operation. With weapons designed upon these principles a high rate of fire is possible. It is interesting to note that the M2 and M3 were specifically designed for tank mounting and were not simply converted field pieces. The sponson mount was designated then standardised as M1.

The M2 gun weighed 783 lb complete, its barrel was 84 inches long and it could, in theory and under test conditions, pierce armour of up to 2½ inches thickness (64 mm) at 500 yards at an angle of 30 degrees to the horizontal. The muzzle velocity was around 1,860 fps which was determined by the round used; the M3 had a higher muzzle velocity of 2,300 fps, it was also heavier weighing in at 910 lb. A crew of two, gunner and loader, served the gun, which could be elevated or depressed by a geared handwheel. Finely geared to one complete turn the gun moved 1 degree 18 minutes. The gun could be traversed also by handgear 14 degrees either way. The gun was electrically fired with a solenoid switch operating the firing trigger. The solenoid button was fitted to the traverse wheel centre. A mechanical firing device was fitted to the mounting for use in case the solenoid switch failed. Later a foot switch was fitted for firing the solenoid. Two hydraulic buffers were fitted to the gun, one over and one below the barrel and breech ring, which controlled the recoil to about 12 inches and returned the gun via internal recuperator springs.

The 37 mm turret gun was developed at Westervliet Arsenal in 1938 for the M2 tank. It came in two versions, the M5 and the M6, the latter being introduced in 1941. The M6 can be identified in its mounting by the cylindrical recuperator housing under the barrel which extends from the front of the mounting, whereas the M5 does not have this. With a muzzle velocity of 2,545 fps, the gun could penetrate 1⅞

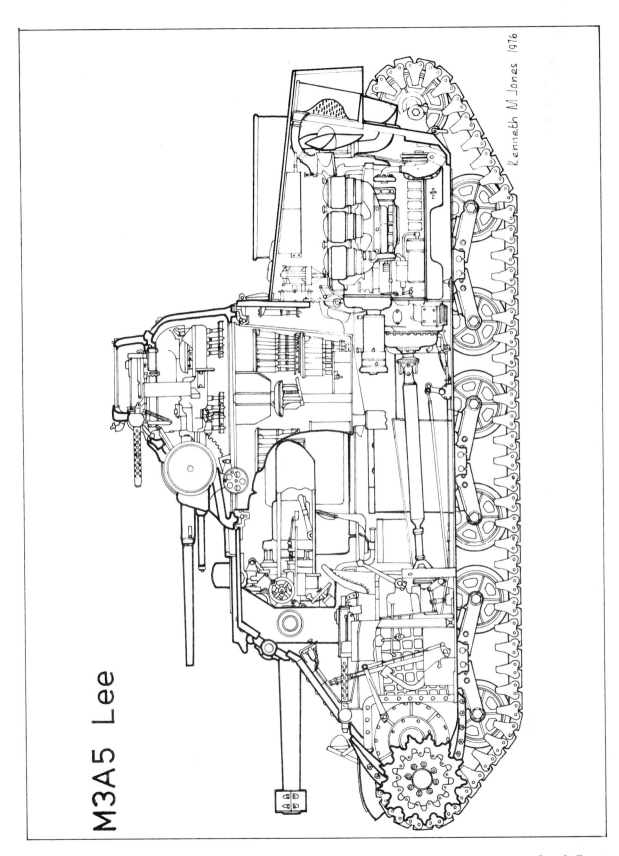

M3A5 Lee

Kenneth M Jones 1976

inches (48 mm) of armour thickness at 500 yards. The gun shared the turret mount with the co-axial .30 cal Browning machine-gun, had a crew of two and was 77 inches long overall. It was fired by solenoid, as the 75 mm gun, or manually if this system failed. By 1941 thicker armour and larger tank guns made this weapon obsolete.

The Royal Armoured Corps established a system of 'parades' for each of its vehicles, to train crews on one basic method of readying their vehicles for battle. The American mediums were no exception and a parade system was evolved for them which was included in the Military Training Pamphlet, No 35, part 20, dated February 1943. This section dealt with the care and maintenance of armament and associated systems. It is interesting to note that the Sherman was in service at the time of its introduction and the British had first used the M3 in action at the so-called Gazala Battle in early 1942. One wonders if the parade system, primarily designed to ensure that the armament was fully operative, was strictly adhered to in the wastes of North Africa, or modified to suit prevailing conditions. It is worth noting that some tank crews could 'go through' a number of tanks during a long battle, provided they got out of their shot-up vehicles and made their way backwards. This also presumed that there were plenty of replacement vehicles for them: a state which improved after the battle of Alamein, when supplies to the 8th Army were intensified, but something that was denied the Afrika Korps, who were always short of war material.

The Parade System was divided into four parades and every crew member, except the commander, had a specified task. The commander would be otherwise engaged, besides he was the one who had to ensure that the tasks were carried out. This system is included here, mainly for its interest to any reader who has not served in any military organisation. When interpreted it will be found that being a tank-man was a full-time business in time of war, and with duties and guards one often wonders when they found time to sleep. This applies especially to those crews in the forward areas, to whom action was always imminent.

The four parades were 'The First Parade', the duration of which was 45 minutes and was held daily; 'The Halt Parade' lasted 30 minutes and was held in conjunction with the midday meal; 'The Last Parade' was of 1½ hours duration and was divided into three parts; finally, a 'Weekly Parade' was held. Time allotted for this was at least five hours.

When the system is examined its merits become plain, especially when it is considered that the crews' lives could depend upon the serviceability of the tank armament, and its engine. The driver would be busy with the care of automative parts, but the gunners and loaders had different tasks on the first parade, held daily. The tasks were divided into two parts, unsheeting and opening up the tank, followed by an inspection of the vehicle and its guns. The gunners' duties were as follows.

The turret gunner, assisted by his loader if he was not on guard or other duties, would remove the breech and muzzle covers of the 37 mm gun, check to see that the gun was unloaded, and make a general examination of the breech mechanism for dirt, rust, cracks or any unserviceabilities. He would lightly oil the frictional surfaces, such as breech blocks or recoil slide, if required. He then had to test the firing gear to check for any defects. The gun mounting was also checked for the tightness of its pins, nuts and bolts, paying particular attention to the coupling of the buffer piston rod to the gun. The gun depression stop, a bolt screwed to the turret beneath the mantlet, was checked for adjustment, otherwise the gun would shoot a piece off the vehicle on full depression. The buffer system was hydraulic, so the cylinder below the gun was checked for its level and any leaks dealt with where possible. The gunner then had to dry-clean the bore if action was expected.

The co-axial machine-gun was checked for the security of its mounting, first, then the firing solenoid checked for action. The bore of this weapon was dry-cleaned before firing. The gunner then checked his M2 periscope sight and his seat fittings and adjustment. A badly seated gunner would have trouble laying and firing, so his seat must be considered an essential part of his equipment if you think how the tank pitched about over uneven terrain with the turret rotating.

The auxiliary weapons, such as the Browning for AA defence in the Grant version and the Thompson .45 sub-machine-gun (one or two were carried — or more!), were checked. The Thompson SMG (then a machine-carbine in British nomenclature) was a standard fitting in the M3s. The tank was delivered with one or two Thompsons stowed as standard along with six hand grenades. This is a point worth remembering by modellers. Guards mounted in leaguer usually equipped themselves with the Thompson, in addition to their pistols. Lee Enfield rifles were not really suited for tank crew use because of length, but their use by tankmen was not unknown.

The stabiliser system was checked by the gunner for oil level in the reservoir, air in the system, and the stiffness control, which was adjusted by the 'hit or miss' methods described in the section on the stabiliser. The traverse system was examined closely. The turret was always given a full rotation by hand gear and twice by power, in both directions, usually when the driver was running up the engine as part of his tasks, because the auxiliary or tank engine had to be running during power-traverse operations to save the drain on the main batteries. The gunner finally checked that all spares and tools were correctly stowed in the tank.

The turret loader would check the turret lights, fan, revolver ports, the protectoscopes and the cupola rotating gear if the M3 was the Lee version. He would check that the 37 mm ammunition was correctly

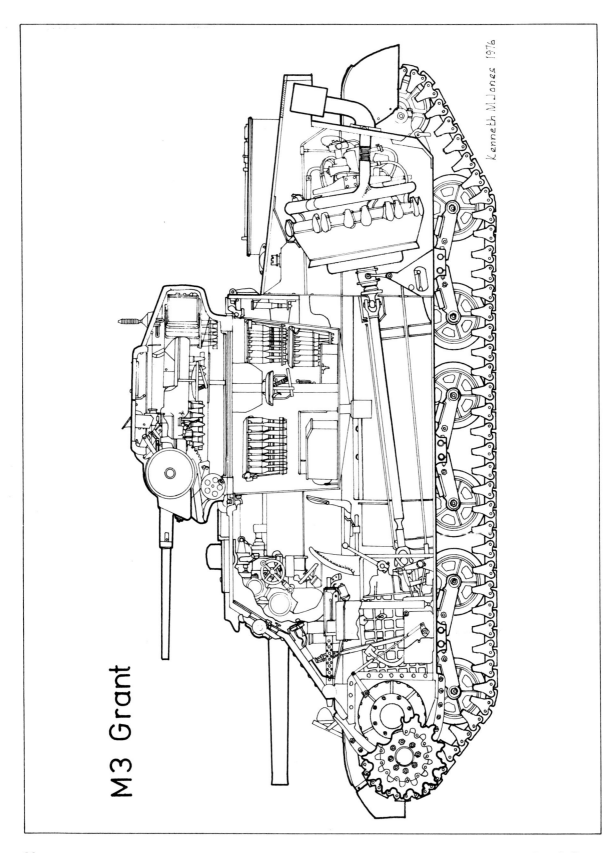

M3 Grant

Kenneth M.Jones 1976

stowed. HE shells Mark II or HE shells M63 were identified by a yellow band, and the M51 armour-piercing rounds by black bands. Any practice rounds carried were painted with blue markings. The 4-inch smoke dischargers on the Lee or the Grant's 2-inch bomb-thrower were also on the gunner's check-list. These were examined for cleanliness and their firing gear checked. The 2-inch bomb-thrower was fired from inside the turret, though the 4-inch dischargers were mounted outside and open to the elements.

The hull gunner and his loader would be busy with the 75 mm gun, doing virtually the same as the turret gunner and his loader. The loader had to check that the ammunition was correctly stowed and that the escape hatch was serviceable.

Ammunition carried in the M3s for the 75 mm gun was — usually — AP M61, coloured black with white markings; AP Mark IT and SAP M72, which were yellow with black markings; and HE M48 Supercharge or HE Mark I normal which were also yellow with black markings. Smoke shells were marked green, though US-supplied smoke shells were grey with a yellow band.

'The Halt Parade' for M3 crews usually coincided with the midday meal whenever possible. During an approach march, or after it, the gunners had to check the guns and gun sights ready for action. All muzzle covers were removed and the fans switched on ready for action. After action had ceased, or during a lull, the 37 mm gunner would check the traverse gear and top up the reservoir if it needed it. He would then check the stabiliser if it had been used in action. Some M3s were delivered minus the stabiliser, or in some cases the crew did not use it, besides the Westinghouse gear, although good in theory, did not always work to satisfaction in practice. Both gunners would check their gun chambers; unload if needed; and clean them, the 37 mm with a brush and the 75 mm breech, being much larger, with a piece of oiled rag. The breech mechanism and the recesses in the breech ring were oiled.

'The Last Parade' was divided into three parts, which were a pre-halt condition report; maintenance; and the crew commander's inspection before closing and camouflaging in harbour. The handbook stated that checks should be carried out in the last 20 minutes before entering harbour. This was easy to estimate in practice but imagine trying to estimate 20 minutes after a full scale battle. Some crews didn't even know where their next harbour would be! In this 20 minutes the turret gunner was instructed to test his seat and sight brow-pad, see that his periscope was secure and check the operation of the guns. The turret loader checked the machine-gun and made a count of rounds fired for replenishment in harbour later on, ensuring that the remaining ammunition was correctly stowed. He also examined the protectoscope, cleaned its prism and checked the operation of the protectoscope shield. The hull gunner and his loaders were performing similar duties in their hull position.

The M3 was halted before positioning in leaguer to enable the driver to make a check of the tracks and running gear. The engine was kept running for the final check of the turret traversing mechanism, sights tested and, if necessary, adjusted by the gunners.

When the tanks were deployed in harbour, all weapons were stripped, cleaned and re-oiled after any firing. Normal daily maintenance for gunners and loaders in the M3 were as follows:

The turret gunner Examine the level of oil in the reservoir of the powered traverse and top up if necessary. Examine the level of oil in the main reservoir of the stabiliser and top up if necessary. Test the stabiliser system for air and bleed the system if it is present. Wipe the 37 mm gun and mounting with an oily rag. Oil the frictional surfaces of the breech mechanism, if they require it. Dry-clean and re-oil the bore. Replace the muzzle cover. Test the action of the AA Browning and Thompson sub-machine-gun and re-oil the working parts if necessary. Dry-clean and re-oil the bore of each weapon.

The turret loader After completing his wireless duties (the turret loader tested the No 19 set in the turret bustle; this consisted of very basic checks to the set), the loader had to clean, test and re-oil the 2-inch bomb thrower (4-inch smoke dischargers on the Lee). He then had to remove all empty ammunition cases and, if needed, replenish the supply. Test all lights. Clean the protectoscope prisms and crew commander's periscope. Clean and leave open all protectoscope shields. Test the rotation of the cupola and re-oil its race if required. Clean the turret floor and see that all spare parts and tools are clean and correctly stowed.

Hull gunner Check the oil level in the reservoir of the stabiliser. Top the system up with oil if the level is below normal. Test the system for air and bleed off if this is present. Wipe the 75 mm gun and its mounting with an oily rag to retard and protect against corrosion. Oil the frictional surfaces of the breech mechanism, dry-clean and re-oil the bore. Replace the muzzle and breech covers to prevent the ingress of dirt and dust.

Hull loader Remove all empty ammunition cases and, if required, replenish the supply. Test the action of the Thompson SMG and re-oil the working parts if necessary. Dry-clean and re-oil the Thompson's bore. Test all lights, the doors and escape hatch. Clean the protectoscope prisms and shields. Leave open the shields, and clean the hull floor. Assist the gunner when these duties are completed.

The driver would be very busy too. He would clean his own vision devices and test his periscopes; check his seat mounting and adjustment, the instruments, gauges and lights on the panel. He would check all oil levels on the transmission and engine components and top up where it was needed. He would report his fuel states and check the supply lines from the tanks to the engine. He would check the tracks and re-lubricate wheel bearings; and clear away any parts of the vehicle — 'battle damaged' — that would be likely·

to foul the running gear in the event of a move at short notice. Everyone was kept pretty busy and had to do a share of guard duty in addition to other fatigues. In the forward areas men would become very tired trying to keep alert with the fear of attack always present.

'The Weekly Parade' for armament was task number six. This dealt specifically with the armament, traverse and the gyro-stabiliser systems. Gunners and loaders were set the following tasks.

75 mm gun and mounting Remove the muzzle and breech covers and see that the gun is unloaded. Strip, dry-clean and examine the breech mechanism for burrs or cracks. Test the action of the firing spring stop and protrusion of the firing pin. Re-oil and reassemble the parts after inspection. Dry-clean, examine and re-oil the bore. Test and, if necessary, adjust the breech closing spring. Clean all parts of the mounting and finally wipe down with an oily rag. Lubricate the operating cam, the nipple on the cradle and those on the elevating and traversing gearboxes. Oil all frictional surfaces and grease the exposed gear teeth. See that all nuts and bolts are to the correct tightness. Ensure that the gun shoulder guard is firmly fixed in position and the bolts are tightened correctly. Examine and replenish, if any is needed, the oil to the required level in the buffer cylinders. Clean and fit the M1 periscope sight.

37 mm gun and mounting Remove the muzzle and breech covers and ensure that the gun is unloaded. Strip, dry-clean and examine the breech mechanism for burrs or cracks. Place the striker unit in the breech block and push it forward to test the action of the firing pin stop and the protrusion of the firing pin. Re-oil and reassemble the parts after inspection. Dry-clean, examine and re-oil the bore. Test the breech closing spring for tension. Clean all parts of the mounting and wipe all over with an oily rag. Lubricate the nipples on the cradle and those on the elevating shaft. Oil all frictional surfaces, especially the semi-automatic cam patch, and grease the exposed gear teeth. See that all nuts, bolts and pins are tight, especially the coupling joining the gun to the buffer piston rod. Check and replenish the oil in the buffer cylinder if the level has decreased. Clean and fit the M2 periscope. See that the depression stop bolt is correctly set.

Co-axial machine-gun and mounting Make certain that the machine-gun is unloaded. Strip the gun, dry-clean and examine the working parts. Lubricate the working parts for action and adjust the cartridge head space (easily accomplished on the M1919A4 Browning; see section on the gun) if adjustment is needed. Dry-clean, examine and re-oil the bore. Reassemble the parts after inspection. Clean all parts of the mounting and place the machine-gun in its position and see that the solenoid bracket is fixed firmly. Finally fit the deflector chute and see that the feed tray is secure.

Tests and adjustments Test and adjust where necessary the firing gear of the 75 mm and 37 mm guns, the seats, sights, lights and fans. Test, clean and lubricate the turret flaps, crew commander's cupola, turret lock, observing periscopes, the sighting vane, the protectoscopes and their shields.

Auxiliary weapons Strip and dry-clean, examine and re-oil the Thompson sub-machine-guns, the AA Browning, smoke weapons and the signal pistol. On the Lee test the firing gear of the 4-inch smoke bomb dischargers and replace their muzzle and breech covers. Check the hand grenades and examine all stowage positions to ensure all auxiliary weapons are properly in place.

Ammunition To obtain consistent shooting, ammunition of the same lot number should be used whenever possible and the 37 mm and 75 mm rounds should be examined as follows. The primer and cap should be clean and undamaged. The cartridge cases should be clean, dry and free from rust and dents. Cracks at the mount of the case not exceeding ¼ inch in length could be ignored, though any cracks elsewhere must condemn the round which should be then rejected.

Projectiles should be dry, clean, well painted and free from cracks or rust. The driving band must be undamaged. Rounds with loose projectiles should be discarded, and ballistic caps where fitted must be secure, otherwise they may become jammed in the bore. HE rounds must be examined for exudation. Gauge rounds in the breech after removing the striker assembly. All ammunition racks and containers should be checked for damage and all rounds correctly stowed.

Boxes of small-arms ammunition must be correctly stowed and the box for the co-axial machine-gun must be firmly fixed on to the carrier. Sealed boxes of ammunition should not be opened until required for immediate use. The AA spools for the Browning should be checked; the Thompson magazines loaded and the inventory of ammunition checked against the numbers allotted to the figures provided for the specific role of the tank.

The interior of the tank was checked for loose articles, waste oil and oily rags and waste which could cause an internal fire. The fire extinguishers were checked for serviceability and security. The gyro-stabiliser and power traverse systems also had to be checked at this stage for oil levels and leakages. The stabiliser system could develop a leak at the packing around the oil pump shaft. All oil and electrical connections were checked and the movement and balance of the guns. On the turret traverse system the nipples were greased on the gearbox and turret ring and all articles likely to affect rotation were removed. The system was then tested manually and on power.

These were the tasks allocated to the crew for the care of the tank's armament as laid down in the training manual. Whether they were strictly adhered to in action really depended on whether there was time, or if there was a strict crew commander or squadron OC. The guns and their care were of paramount importance, since badly maintained guns did not operate correctly or shoot straight and constantly gave trouble. Wear in the bore of both guns was unavoidable during firing because of friction set up by the driving band of the projectile and the heat set up by the propellant-charge. Incorrect cleaning or neglect could also cause wear. To maintain a good bore, daily cleaning and leaving the bore oily when the gun was not in use was advised. A highly polished bore minimises the tendency to rust and metallic fouling forming. As the bore wears, greater care is needed to prevent corrosion.

It is easy to imagine the difficulties of trying to keep a gun barrel clean in North Africa. The effect of sand and dust in weapons can be pictured easily. The manual stated that in sandy countries oil was to be used very sparingly. In cold weather or climates with temperatures below zero, cold test number 1 had to be used as a lubricant. At extremely low temperatures, 20 per cent paraffin had to be added to all lubricants.

SAE 30 oil was used to oil the M3's gun bores, breech mechanism, slides and outer surfaces. All gun gearwheels and trunnion bearings were greased monthly to ensure smooth action. The breech closing chain spring had to be greased weekly. It was stressed to all crews that over-lubrication caused the accumulation of dust.

Fouling of the bores on both 37 mm and 75 mm guns of the M3 was a major contributor to a reduction in 'life expectancy'. There are three types of fouling: superficial, internal and metallic. Superficial fouling is caused by the waste product left from the propellant charge adhering to the surface of the bore. If this is allowed to form, it encourages rust; if left for a long time it hardens and produces effects similar to internal fouling or pitting. Dry-cleaning and oiling of the bore after firing removes superficial fouling from the bore.

Internal fouling is hard to detect in weapons. It is caused by waste combustion products being absorbed into the metal through its pores. If this fouling is neglected after discovery it will eventually be forced from the pores of the metal and form a hard black crust on the surface of the bore. Only a certain amount of this fouling can be got rid of by boiling water and daily scouring until sweating ceases from the deposits in the bore.

Metallic fouling is caused by small pieces from the driving band being left on the surface of the bore. It appears as copper streaks on the bands and in the grooves of the rifling. This problem, and its removal, was a specialist task and was not done by the gunner but by a gun-fitter. Bore cleaning for 37 mm and 75 mm guns was advised daily, before and after any firing. Daily, their bores had to be cleaned with the brush and oiled with the slush brush drawn through the bore. Before firing, or anticipated action, the bore and chamber had to be dry-cleaned with a piece of rag wrapped around the bore brush.

After firing, the bore and chamber had to be dry-cleaned and oiled to remove superficial fouling and, where possible, the bore scoured with boiling water to remove any internal fouling. This was done on both guns by placing an empty shell case in the chamber, closing the breech, elevating the gun and partially filling the bore with boiling water and scouring it with the sponge and staff. The gun was then depressed to drain off the water, which in North Africa was no doubt caught in a can and boiled up again for future use.

Depicting the cleaning of armament in a model diorama using the Airfix Lee or Grant would make an attractive display if 1:32 scale figures were shown sponging out the bore and cleaning the machine-guns, just as on the original. It is hoped that the procedures described in reproducing these armament maintenance notes from the handbook will give some ideas which can be put to use by the modeller.

Browning machine-guns

Included in the M3's design were four .30-calibre Browning machine-guns, which appeared to have been a 'throwback' from the M2 mediums which absolutely bristled with machine-guns. Four were mounted in barbettes at the corners of the hull; again, this went back to the World War 1 concept of crossing enemy trenches and firing down into them with

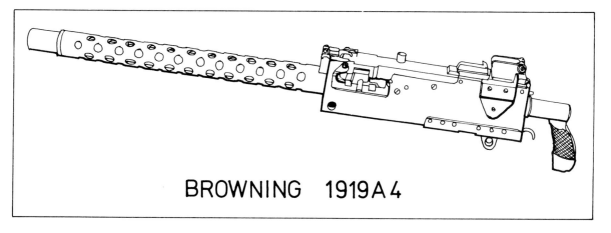

BROWNING 1919A4

machine-guns where the main armement would be unable to bear. The M2 medium was designed with deflector plates over the rear track guards, just over the idler, to enable the two rear machine-guns to fire a fusilade of shots which would be deflected downwords. This was the theory, anyway: whether it would have worked in practice is another matter. The M2 never saw combat, and the ideas of static trench warfare were rarely encountered in World War 2.

The M3 Lee mounted two fixed Brownings in the hull front on the left side. Another Browning shared a co-axial mounting (the M24 mounting) with the 37 mm gun which, along with this weapon, could be gyro-stabilised in use. On the turret top the fully rotating cupola mounted another Browning within its cramped interior. The Grant was not fitted with this cupola, although a Browning was carried inside the tank to be mounted as an anti-aircraft weapon on the cupola ring. Compared to contemporary British, German and Soviet tanks, the M3 had a heavy secondary armament.

The Browning M1919 appeared in six versions, from the basic M1919 to the M1919A6 — which was not a tank gun, but an attempt to produce a light machine-gun version (or, more correctly, fitting the M1919A4 version with flash eliminator, bipod and butt).

The original M1919 was developed for tanks from the M1917 water-cooled gun, itself designed by John Browning, an American citizen who found that more interest in his designs was taken by the warlike Europeans; he moved to Fabarique Nationale in Belgium where many of his designs were produced.

The Brownings fitted to the M3 mediums were mainly M1919A4 and M1919A5 versions of the gun. The M1919A4 was an improved M1919A2. The barrel was lengthened from 18.63 inches to 24 inches, and the M1919 was produced as a fixed gun from the M1919A4 for fitting into gyro-stabilised co-axial mountings and the cupola on the Lee with its limited dimensions. The tactical value of this cupola was negligible and was often removed in British service. Usually the Browning gun was removed as it could not be elevated fully with the cupola hatch open. The fumes from the gun whilst firing within the confines of the cupola can be imagined, especially if the cupola hatch was shut. A hatch stop was fitted to the cupola on later model Lees to stop the hatch flap from coming into contact with the machine-gun barrel where it would have damaged the air-cooled casing.

The M1919A4s fitted to the tank could be dismantled for action outside the tank and a tripod was issued — strapped to the hull — for this purpose. In British service the two fixed hull guns were usually removed, retaining only the co-axial gun and the anti-aircraft weapon.

The M1919A5 version of the gun was modified specifically for co-axial mountings which entailed fitting re-designed features, though basically the gun

was an M1919A4. The sights were removed as the gun was sighted via the 37 mm telescope, where provision was made for its independent use. The cocking handle was removed and replaced by a stud which was actuated by a custom-designed charging slide handle fitted to the right-hand side plate of the gun. The cartridges were belt-fed into the left-hand side of the gun by a fabric belt of 50, 100, 150 or 250 rounds capacity.

Three types of ammunition were available for use in the Browning: an armour-piercing round which was identified by a green or black bullet tip; a tracer which had red markings; or the standard ball ammunition which was not colour-coded.

The M1919A5 was solenoid-fired in the co-axial mount. The standard M1919A4 backplate with its pistol grip and trigger assembly was removed and replaced by the solenoid backplate which was wired to the trigger switch on the gunner's spade grip control, from where the Browning was fired.

The M1919A4 mounted in the cupola could not carry the standard backplate with the pistol grip and trigger, so it used the M1919 aircraft gun backplate with a vertical buffer. A special trigger mechanism was mounted below and along the left-hand side of the gun. This was a remote mechanical linkage bolted to the gun with a single nut and bolt, and could be quickly removed from the gun. The gun in this position needed a deflector chute to carry the empty cartridge cases downwards. The machine-gun was provided with a locking device — a simple sprung plunger — which engaged a bracket on the cupola wall to lock it when not in use.

The Brownings were recoil-operated weapons, firing fully automatic only and belt-fed. Recoil operation is where the force of the detonating cartridge forces a locked barrel and bolt backwards, unlocking them and allowing the barrel to return to battery and the bolt to continue in a rearwards direction against the mainspring which compresses it. As the bolt moves rearwards a transporter strips a live round from the belt and places it in a 'T' slot in the block face, ejecting the fired round from its slot in the block face out of the gun. The new round is chambered by the bolt which locks itself to the barrel and its striker fires the next round, repeating the firing cycle once again.

The Browning was reliable and had a reasonable rate of fire, around 500 rounds per minute, making it well suited to tank use. Two versions of the M1919A4 were fitted to M3s, the 'fixed' and 'flexible' versions. The fixed versions were fitted into cupolas and co-axial mounts and the flexible versions — ie those with a pistol grip — were fitted into the bow. The cartridge head space was easily adjusted on the Browning, not usually a simple operation on machine-guns. The cartridge head space is the space between the bolt face and the periphery of the barrel extension that is the barrel face or chamber. The head space adjustment is critical in the operation of the weapon: if the gap is

Lee & Grant

too large the cartridge case will move backwards, causing a probable rupture of the case; if it is too small the gun will not fire because of safety measures built into the weapon. The head space could be adjusted by operating a ratchet on the barrel moving it backwards or forwards to adjust the gap, a feature very suited on this weapon to field adjustment, especially in action.

Browning M1919A4 (fixed and flexible)

Calibre: .30 in (7.62 mm)
Overall length: 40.9 in (104 cm)
Barrel length: 24 in (61 cm)
Weight: 30.86 lb (14 kg)
Effective range: 984 yards (900 m)
Operation: Recoil — fully automatic only
Muzzle velocity: 2,788 ft per sec (850 m/sec)
Sights: Front blade, rear leaf 1
    (M1919A5 no sights; M24 combination mount
    telescope used)
Feed: Fabric belt 50, 100, 150, 250
Cyclic rate: 400 - 500 rpm

Data	M2
Crew	6
Weight	38,000 lbs (17,252 kg)
Length	17 ft 6 in (533 cm)
Height	9 ft 4½ in (285.75 cm)
Width	8 ft 6 in (259 cm)
Track width	13 in (33 cm)
Track centres	6 ft 9 in (205.74 cm)
Armament	1 x 37 mm M5/M6 and 8 x .30 cal MGs
Ammunition stowage	200 37 mm rounds and 12,250 .30 MG rounds
Maximum speed	26 mph (42 kph)
Cross-country speed	17.2 mph (27.5 kph)
Crusing range	130 miles (208 km)
Step	2 ft (60.9 cm)
Trench	7 ft 6 in (228.6 cm)

The hulls of the M2 and M2A1 were part riveted and part welded. These tanks were entirely hand-built, being before the days of mass production, and although the M2A1 was earmarked for mass production at Detroit it was cancelled in favour of the M3 design. The turrets were of welded construction. The angled plates over the rear track guards were to deflect machine-gun fire — from the two rear hull barbettes — down into any trench that the tank crossed: a novel throw-back from World War 1 experience.

The M2 can be distinguished from the M2A1 by the different turrets, the latter being vertical sided, and the splash plates on the M2A1's glacis. The M2A1 also had an armoured 37 mm gun mantlet. The M2's chassis, virtually unchanged, became standard on both the M3 and the M4.

M2 and variants

M2 — First production type in 1939.
M2A1 — Second production type in 1940-1941.
M2 with E2 flame-gun — Test vehicle for flame-throwing trials in 1941. A long flame-gun was mounted in place of the 37 mm gun and the fuel containers were mounted on the hull rear.

Development vehicles

T5 (later T5 Phase I) was the prototype for the series in 1938. A T5 Phase II vehicle was projected with an alternative engine but never materialised. The T5 Phase III was re-engined with a Wright radial aero-engine as production prototype for the M2. The T5E1 was the pilot model with a Guiberson radial diesel engine and was used as a test installation for twin 37 mm guns. T5E2 was a T5 Phase III vehicle converted with a modified hull and mounted a 75 mm howitzer and rangefinder turret. The 75 mm howitzer was mounted in a sponson on the right hull front, the configuration adopted for the M3 mediums. The British type of turret fitted to the Grant was test-installed on an M2 medium at Rock Island.

Data	M2A1
Crew	6
Weight	47,040 lbs (21,356 kg)
Length	17 ft 6 in (533 cm)
Height	9 ft 3 in (281.9 cm)
Width	8 ft 6 in (259 cm)
Track width	14 in (35.5 cm)
Track centres	6 ft 9 in (205.74 cm)
Armament	1 x 37 mm M5/M6 and 8 x .30 cal MGs
Ammunition stowage	200 37 mm rounds and 12,250 .30 MG rounds
Maximum speed	26 mph (42 kph)
Cross-country speed	17.2 mph (27.5 kph)
Cruising range	130 miles (208 km)
Step	2 ft (60.9 cm)
Trench	7 ft 6 in (228.6 cm)

M3 Production Variants

M3 — Initial production model from April to August 1941 onwards. Riveted construction, with side doors and a Wright Continental radial aero-engine. Built at Detroit Arsenal, Chrysler (3,243), American Locomotive (385), Baldwin (295), Pressed Steel (501) and Pullman (500). Total output to August 1942 was 4,924.
M3A1 — Identical vehicle to the M3 in automotive parts, but had a cast hull built only by American Locomotive, who produced 300 from February to August 1942. Late production M3A1s had no hull doors and an escape hatch in the hull floor instead.
M3A2 — Mechanically identical to the M3 but with an all-welded construction which was thought to be superior to riveted vehicles. Baldwin built only 12 tanks commencing in January 1942 then ceased pro-

Above *M31 with dummy gun lifting an M4 (76 mm) from a ditch.*
Left *Gun Motor Carriage T6.* **Below left** *40 mm Gun Motor Carriage T36.*

duction of the M3A2 in favour of the M3A3.

M3A3 — All-welded hull as the M3A2 but fitted with the General Motors 6-71 twin diesels which increased its top speed to 29 mph. This variant was built by Baldwin between March and December 1942. Production total was 322. Side doors were omitted or welded up on later models.

M3A4 — This variant was fitted with the Chrysler-developed A57 Multibank engine. Built only at Detroit Arsenal between June and August 1942. The hull had to be extended to take the new engine increasing the weight to 64,000 lbs. 109 vehicles were built.

M3A5 — Identical to M3A3 but the hull was riveted not welded. Built by Baldwin between January and November 1942. Production total was 591.

Special purpose variants

Mine Exploder TI (for M3 Medium) — This was a mine-exploding attachment consisting of a twin disc roller and a single disc roller pushed and trailed by the tank. Developed by Chrysler for the M3 medium in 1942. Not successful in service.

M3 with E3 flame-gun — This was developed from the E2 flame-gun fitted to the M2 medium but was used in trials only in 1942. The flame-gun was mounted in the turret in place of the 37 mm gun. The 75 mm gun was also removed.

M3 with E5R2-M3 flame-gun — This was a portable flame-thrower supplied for attachment in the field. It came as a kit and was fitted in the machine-gun cupola on the Lee turret.

RA PD 66694

Shop Tractor T10 — A US version of the British Canal Defence Light. 355 production models on mainly the M3A1 chassis. These were built by American Locomotive between May and December 1943 and were not used in action.

Heavy Tractor T16 — This was an artillery tractor. It was the standard M3 with the turret and main armament removed. It had a large winch fitted but it was not used because of limited interior space.

Tank Recovery Vehicle T2 (M31) — This was an M3 with the guns removed and a rear-mounted boom fitted, with a winch and large stowage box installed. The T2 was redesignated M31 in September 1943. The M31B1 was the T2 configuration on the M3A3 tank and the M31B2 based on the M3A5.

Fully Tracked Prime Mover M33 — This was the M31 ARV further converted as a tractor for the 155 mm gun. The boom and turret were removed and an air compressor and outlet pipes fitted for gun carriage braking systems. A .50 cal AA machine-gun was fitted on the hull top. The M44 was similar but had a cupola on top of the hull sponson.

Right *3-inch Gun Motor Carriage T24.* **Below** *3-inch Gun Motor Carriage T40/M9.*

The Lee and Grant in detail

Above Grant OP/Command tank. **Below** *Grant Scorpion III being loaded on to an LCT.*

3-inch Motor Carriage T24 — This was an attempt to mount a 3-inch gun on the M3 chassis. The turret and 75 mm gun sponson were removed. The project was cancelled as unsuitable.

3-inch Gun Motor Carriage T40 (M9) — This mounted the M1918 3-inch anti-aircraft gun as a tank destroyer. This project was cancelled in favour of the M10 GMC in August 1942 as insufficient guns could be obtained for a production batch.

40 mm Gun Motor Carriage T36 — This was a 40 mm anti-aircraft gun fitted in a fully rotating turret but it proved too complex and was cancelled after tests.

The M3 was used as a test bed for the Ford GAA engines for Shermans as the M3E1. The M3A1E1 was fitted with three 6-cylinder Lycoming engines. The M3A5E1 was used to test Hydra-matic transmissions, in a twin configuration. The M3A5E2 was used to test single Hydra-matic transmission. An M3A4 was used to test sprung idler wheels and horizontal volute spring suspension system.

British service variants

Grant I — M3 with turret to British requirements.

Grant II — British designation for United States M3A5 with the Lee turret.

Lee I — British designation for M3 Medium with Lee turret.

Lee II — British designation for M3A1 Medium with Lee turret.

Lee III — British designation for M3A2 Medium. Not supplied to Britain.

Lee IV — British designation for M3A3 with Continental engine.

Lee V — British designation for M3A3 with diesel engine.

Lee VI — British designation for M3A4.

Grant ARV — British conversion of Grant I or II. The guns were removed and a towing winch fitted with an 'A' frame hoist that could be attached to the front for limited light aid recoveries. Some had a twin Bren anti-aircraft mount.

Grant ARV 1 — British designation for the United States-built T2 ARV (M31).

Below left *Side view of Grant ARV I.* **Below** *Grant Scorpion IV.*

Lee & Grant

Above left *Grant ARV I from above. Note twin Bren machine-guns for AA defence.* **Above right** *Rear view of Grant ARV showing stowage of recovery equipment.* **Below** *Grant CDL.*

Priest Kangaroo.

Grant Command Tank — This was a Grant fitted with map table and extra radio equipment for command work. Armament was sometimes removed.

Grant Scorpion III — This was a mine flail tank. The 75 mm gun was removed to clear the flails and a counter-weight was fitted to the rear. The flail was driven by a Bedford engine on the rear to work the flail motor.

Grant Scorpion IV — This was identical to the Scorpion III but had two flail motors fitted instead of only one.

Grant CDL — The turret was replaced by a purpose-built light projector armoured turret. The 75 mm gun was retained for the offensive rôle, and a Besa machine-gun was fitted in the light projector turret.

M7 Priest Howitzer Motor Carriage — This was an M3 chassis with a 105 mm howitzer fitted into a purpose-built open-topped fighting compartment.

M3 Medium tank of the 2nd Armoured Division, French Army, in Normandy.

The vehicle was called 'Priest' by the British because of the machine-gun cupola's resemblance to a church pulpit. The M7 was built by the American Locomotive Company and Pressed Steel Corporation.

Data	M7 Priest
Crew:	7
Weight loaded:	50,639 lbs (22,970 kg)
Length:	19 ft 9 in (601.9 cm)
Width:	9 ft 5½ in (287.8 cm)
Height:	9 ft 8 in (294.6 cm) (inc AA MG)
Ground clearance:	17⅛ in (43.5 cm)
Track centres:	83 in (210.8 cm)
Ground contact:	147 in (373.38 cm)
Ground pressure:	10.38 lb/sq in (.73 kg/sq cm)
Max road speed:	25 mph (40 kph)
Range:	87 to 125 miles (140 to 201 km) cross-country and road
Fuel capacity:	149 gallons (677 litres)
Ford:	4 ft (121.9 cm)
Gradient:	60%
Step:	2 ft (60.9 cm)
Trench:	7 ft 6 in (228.6 cm)
Engine:	Continental R-975-C1 9-cylinder radial petrol air-cooled developing 350 hp at 2,400 rpm
Armament:	1 x 105 mm Howitzer M2A1 (M1A2 and M2 also); elevation + 35°, depression −5°, traverse 30° left, 15° right; and 1 x .50 cal (12.7 mm) M2 HB MG for anti-aircraft use
Armour:	Hull

front upper	½ in (12.7 mm)
front lower	2-4½ in (50-114 mm)
sides upper	½ in (12.7 mm)
sides lower	1½ in (38 mm)
rear upper	½ in (12.7 mm)
rear lower	1 in (25.4 mm)
bottom front	1 in (25.4 mm)
rear	½ in (12.7 mm)

The M7 was developed from the 105 mm Howitzer Motor Carriage T32. Production commenced June 1941. The two pilot models built by Baldwin were standardised as the M7 in February 1942. 4,267 M7s and variants were built between 1942 and 1945 by American Locomotive (M7), Pressed Steel (M7/M7B1) and Federal Machine & Welder (M7B2). This vehicle was replaced by the Sexton in British service.

M3 Medium technical data
(United States and British service Lee)

ARMAMENT
One 75 mm M2 or M3 gun in M1 sponson mounting.

One 37 mm M5 or M6 gun in M24 combination turret mounting.

One .30 cal Browning machine-gun M1919A4 co-axial in M24 turret mounting.

One .30 cal Browning machine-gun M1919A4 in cupola on turret.

Two .30 cal Browning machine-guns M1919A4 fixed forward-firing in hull glacis.

One .45 cal Thompson sub-machine-gun. Crew personal weapon (plus pistols, etc).

AMMUNITION STOWAGE

75 mm:	46 rounds
37 mm:	178 rounds
Calibre .30:	9,200 rounds
Calibre .45:	1,200 rounds
Hand grenades:	12

T.32 pilot model for the Howitzer Motor Carriage M7.

ARMOUR

Hull —	Actual	Basis
Front upper:	2 in (51 mm)	4⅜ in (111 mm)
Lower:	1½ in (38 mm)	2¾ in (70 mm)
Sides:	1½ in (38 mm)	1½ in (38 mm)
Rear:	1½ in (38 mm)	1⅝ in (42 mm)
Top:	½ in (13 mm)	
Bottom:	1-½ in (26-13 mm)	
Turret —		
Front:	2¼ in (57 mm)	6½ in (165 mm)
Sides and rear:	2¼ in (57 mm)	2 in (51 mm)
Top:	⅞ in (22 mm)	

VISION AND FIRE CONTROL

Periscope M1:	one (75 mm gun)
Periscope M3:	one (37 mm gun)
Protectoscopes:	seven (hull and turret)

COMMUNICATIONS

Radio (with intercom):	SCR - 508.
Radio in command tanks:	SCR - 506.

Battery: 24 volts.

FIRE FIGHTING EQUIPMENT

Fixed 10 lb CO_2 extinguishers: 2.
Hand-operated 4 lb CO_2 extinguishers: 2.

TRANSMISSION

Type: fully synchromesh, 5 forward, 1 reverse.
  Gear ratios:

First gear: 7.56:1	Fourth gear: 1.11:1
Second gear: 3.11:1	Fifth gear: 0.73:1
Third gear: 1.78:1	Reverse: 5.65:1

  Controlled differential gear ratio: 3.53:1
  Steering ratio: 1.515:1

FINAL DRIVE

Type: Herringbone.
Gear ratio: 2.84:1.
Sprocket teeth: 13.
Pitch diameter: 25.038.

105 mm Howitzer Motor Carriage M7, first production model.

SUSPENSION

Type: Vertical volute spring.
Wheel size (tyre size): 20 x 9.
Idler, adjustable eccentric, size: 22 x 9.

TRACK

Type: Rubber block, dry pinned.
Width: 16 in (421 mm).
Pitch: 6 in (152.5 mm).
Shoes per track: 158, 166 on M3A4.

British ammunition stowage for Grant and Lee
(RAC Pamphlet No 35, Part 20)

	Lee	Grant
75 mm:	65	65 rounds
37 mm:	126	139 rounds
.30 cal:	4,000	4,000 rounds

.45 cal:	640 (32 x 20 round magazines)	640 rounds
Grenades:	6	6
Very pistol:	12 (4 red, 4 green, 4 illuminating)	12
2-inch bomb thrower:		14 bombs
4-inch smoke discharger:	8 (Smoke bombs and Ballistite cartridges)	

The above stowage was often increased in action for obvious reasons, and is only the recommended official stowage.

The Grant was as for the M3 riveted except that some had radial Guiberson diesels, were 9 feet 3 inches high (281.94 cm), and were fitted with the British No 19 radio set which was installed in the turret bustle.

Technical specifications M3 Medium production models, Lee

	M3 riveted	M3A1 cast	M3A2 welded	M3A3 welded	M3A4 riveted	M3A5 riveted
Weight:	60,000 lbs (27,240 kg)	60,000 lbs (27,240 kg)	60,000 lbs (27,240 kg)	63,000 lbs (28,602 kg)	64,000 lbs (29,056 kg)	64,000 lbs (29,056 kg)
Length:	18 ft 6 in (563.88 cm)	18 ft 6 in (563.88 cm)	18 ft 6 in (563.88 cm)	18 ft 6 in (563.88 cm)	19 ft 8 in (599.44 cm)	18 ft 6 in (563.88 cm)
Width:	8 ft 11 in (271.78 cm)	8 ft 11 in (271.78 cm)	8 ft 11 in (271.78 cm)	8 ft 11 in (271.78 cm)	8 ft 11 in (271.78 cm)	8 ft 11 in (271.78 cm)
Height:	10 ft 3 in (312.42 cm)	10 ft 3 in (312.42 cm)	10 ft 3 in (312.42 cm)	10 ft 3 in (312.42 cm)	10 ft 3 in (312.42 cm)	10 ft 3 in (312.42 cm)
Turret ring inside diameter:	57 in (144.78 cm)	57 in (144.78 cm)	57 in (144.78 cm)	57 in (144.78 cm)	57 in (144.78 cm)	57 in (144.78 cm)
Ground clearance:	17⅛ in (43.5 cm)	17⅛ in (43.5 cm)	17⅛ in (43.5 cm)	17⅛ in (43.5 cm)	17⅛ in (43.5 cm)	17⅛ in (43.5 cm)
Track centres:	83 in (210.8 cm)	83 in (210.8 cm)	83 in (210.8 cm)	83 in (210.8 cm)	83 in (210.8 cm)	83 in (210.8 cm)
Ground contact:	147 in (373.38 cm)	147 in (373.38 cm)	147 in (373.38 cm)	147 in (373.38 cm)	160 in (406.4 cm)	147 in (373.38 cm)
Ground pressure:	13.36 lb/sq in (.94 kg/sq cm)	13.36 lb/sq in (.94 kg/sq cm)	13.36 lb/sq in (.94 kg/sq cm)	13.36 lb/sq in (.94 kg/sq cm)	12.9 lb/sq in (.9 kg/sq cm)	13.36 lb/sq in (.94 kg/sq cm)
Maximum speed:	26 mph (42 kph)	26 mph (42 kph)	26 mph (42 kph)	29 mph (46 kph)	26 mph (42 kph)	29 mph (46 kph)
Maximum gradient:	60%	60%	60%	60%	60%	60%
Trench:	6 ft 2½ in (189.3 cm)	6 ft 2½ in (189.3 cm)	6 ft 2½ in (189.3 cm)	6 ft 2½ in (189.3 cm)	6 ft 2½ in (189.3 cm)	6 ft 2½ in (189.3 cm)
Vertical step:	2 ft (60.9 cm)	2 ft (60.9 cm)	2 ft (60.9 cm)	2 ft (60.9 cm)	2 ft (60.9 cm)	2 ft (60.9 cm)
Fording depth:	40 in (101.6 cm)	40 in (101.6 cm)	40 in (101.6 cm)	36 in (91.44 cm)	40 in (101.6 cm)	40 in (101.6 cm)
Fuel capacity:	175 gallons (795.55 litres)	175 gallons (795.55 litres)	175 gallons (795.55 litres)	150 gallons (681.9 litres)	160 gallons (727.36 litres)	175 gallons (795.55 litres)
Cruising range:	120 miles (192 km)	120 miles (192 km)	120 miles (192 km)	160 miles (256 km)	120 miles (192 km)	160 miles (256 km)
Turning circle:	37 ft (11.28 metres)	37 ft (11.28 metres)	37 ft (11.28 metres)	37 ft (11.28 metres)	39 ft (11.88 metres)	37 ft (11.28 metres)
Engine make: Model: Type:	Continental R975 EC2 or C1 Radial air-cooled	Continental R975 EC2 or C1 Radial air-cooled	Continental R975 EC2 or C1 Radial air-cooled	General Motors 6-71 6046 Twin in-line liquid-cooled	Chrysler A-57 Multi-bank liquid-cooled	General Motors 6-71 6046 Twin in-line liquid-cooled
Cylinders:	9	9	9	12 (6 × 2)	30 (6 × 5)	12 (6 × 2)
Fuel octane/ cetane:	92 or 80 gasoline	92 or 80 gasoline	92 or 80 gasoline	50 diesel	80 gasoline	50 diesel
Max governed speed:	2,400 rpm	2,400 rpm	2,400 rpm	2,100 rpm	2,400 rpm	2,100 rpm
Brake Horse Power:	340	340	340	375	370	375
Maximum torque:	800 ft/lb (110.7 mkg) at 1,800 rpm	800 ft/lb (110.7 mkg) at 1,800 rpm	800 ft/lb (110.7 mkg) at 1,800 rpm	1,000 ft/lb (138.4 mkg) at 1,400 rpm	1,020 ft/lb (141.1 mkg) at 1,200 rpm	1,000 ft/lb (138.4 mkg) at 1,400 rpm

Lee & Grant

Chapter Three

Camouflage and markings

In its short service life the M3 bore various types of camouflage and markings, ranging from the early semi-gloss green of the US Army, along with colourful markings to the light matt sandy colours applied by the British in North Africa.

United States of America

The M3s were first painted in dark green and were marked with the prominent three-colour national insignia more commonly associated with aircraft, a white star on a blue background with a red central spot within the star. These stars were painted on the hull sides and front plate. White company identification digits were painted on the turret and repeated on the front plate, usually the company letter followed by the tank's individual number within the company. The War Department number was painted on to the hull sides, at the rear alongside the engine compartment. The serial number was prefixed by the letters, USA — W in a bluish-grey called blue drab, but these numbers were also painted in off-white and yellow.

Later the colour olive drab became standard and there was an officially recommended scheme combining this with black to form a disruptive pattern. Recommended schemes were also available for desert and arctic theatres. Despite these official schemes, overall drab colours were more usual, olive being the more common finish, though on some vehicles this was given a little contrast by the colourful insignia of the United States Armoured Divisions painted on to the glacis. Personal vehicle names in white were also very prevalent.

When the Americans brought their M3 Lees to the United Kingdom prior to Operation Torch, they appeared in overall olive drab with blue drab WD numbers, and plain white stars on the turrets with white bars marked right around the turret walls. The company letter and tank number was painted on the armoured centre panel of the transmission casing. A large number of the tanks were named in small white letters on a slant following the line of the hull side

Grant with lorry camouflage tilt.

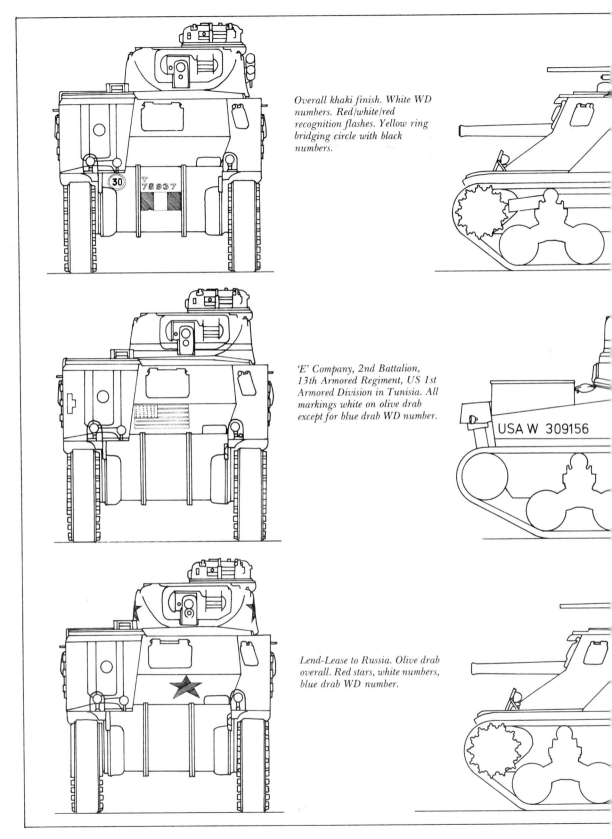

Overall khaki finish. White WD numbers. Red/white/red recognition flashes. Yellow ring bridging circle with black numbers.

'E' Company, 2nd Battalion, 13th Armored Regiment, US 1st Armored Division in Tunisia. All markings white on olive drab except for blue drab WD number.

Lend-Lease to Russia. Olive drab overall. Red stars, white numbers, blue drab WD number.

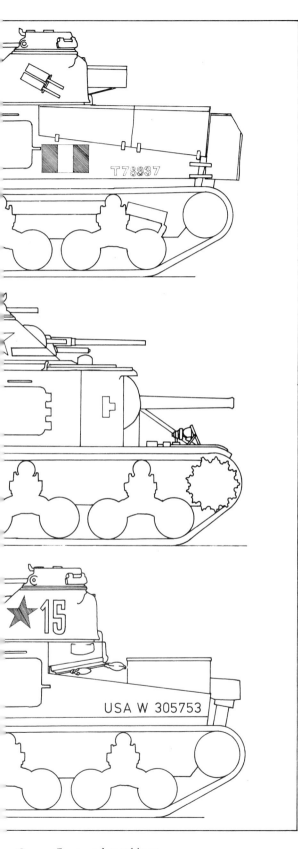

plate behind the hull doors. A geometrically styled motif appeared on either side of the hull, on the 75 mm gun sponson and the front angled side plate which related to the tank's company, battalion, and regiment within the division. A number denoted the tank's individual number within its company.

Vehicles went to North Africa in the above guise, with the outlines of the flag of the United States of America stencilled on in white only. The American crewmen were quick to emulate their German counterparts in splashing their vehicles with wet mud, allowing it to dry into a camouflage coating. The Americans treated their olive-painted vehicles just as the Germans treated Panzer grey on arrival in the Western Desert.

Great Britain

The first M3s received by the British, both Grants and Lees, were required for service in the North African theatre. Save for a handful kept in Britain, perhaps for training, evaluation or even propaganda purposes, all went to the desert direct from American arsenals; these were, of course, finished olive drab. On arrival in the Western Desert they were fitted with British-designed sand-shields and camouflage screen stringers were welded along the hull at workshops. The olive drab was overpainted light stone and some tanks were given a pattern of darker stripes to break up the high-sided outline. British War Department numbers, prefixed 'T' for tank, were painted in white on the olive drab and when the vehicle was painted stone these were masked off leaving a rectangular strip of olive drab with the white figures showing. Alternatively the WD numbers were re-painted in black or grey on to the hull sides over the stone. Some Grants can be seen in a stone and brown, green or slate camouflage with darker brown or black edging to the brown. Finally, in 1943, light mud with blue/black and all undersides of guns, undercuts of turrets, etc, in white, became the official scheme.

Standard British markings were painted on to the M3s if time allowed. Some Lees operated in plain sand devoid of any marks, even WD numbers. Their place in the line of battle was more important than a coat of paint or a few markings. The large red-white-red recognition patches were sometimes painted on, along with the squadron marking on the turret: this was a geometric motif, and could contain a troop number within its outline. Arm of service and divisional signs appeared on the front dust guards or on the transmission housings, the latter being regarded as a more permanent location, since the former had a habit of being blown away, or falling off. These markings could be — but were not always — emblazoned on the rear plate. Really it was a case of how long the crew had to paint such markings on, or often dictated by the discipline and 'bull' in a unit which still seemed to be omni-present even in wartime.

The arm of service marking, about 8½″ × 9½″ in dimensions, identified the tank's regiment within its

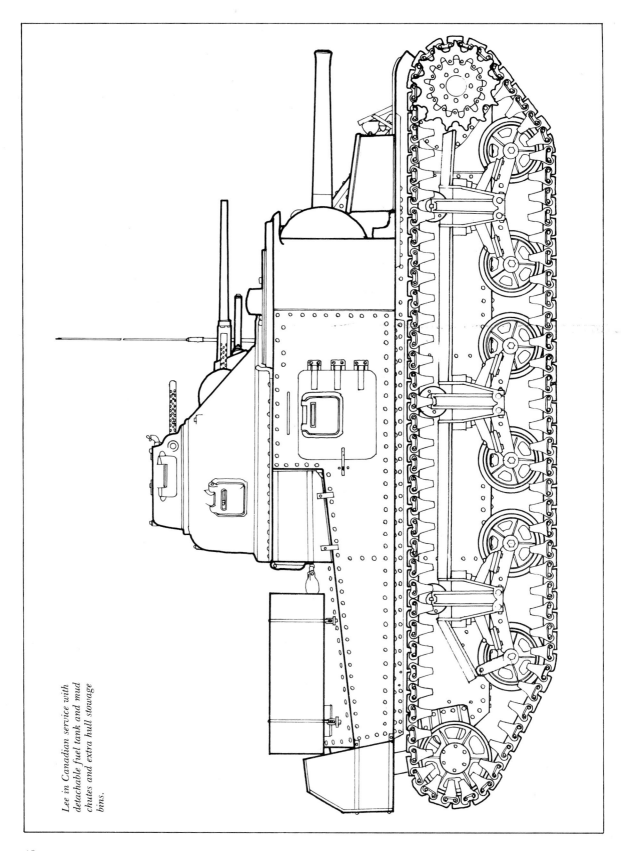

Lee in Canadian service with detachable fuel tank and mud chutes and extra hull stowage bins.

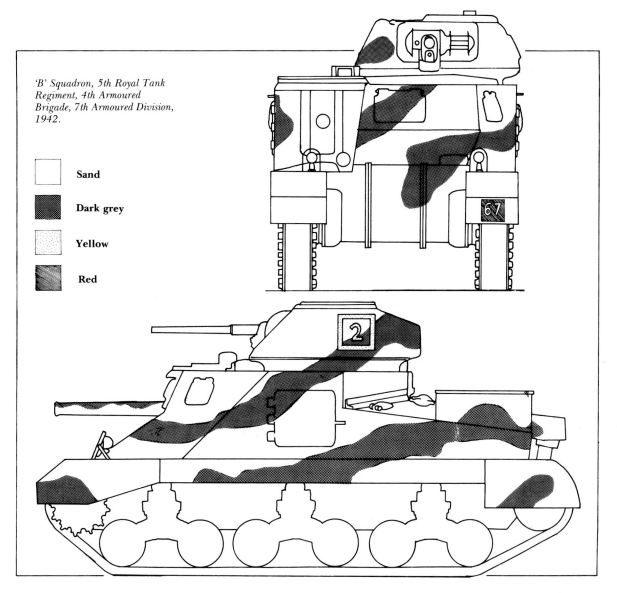

'B' Squadron, 5th Royal Tank Regiment, 4th Armoured Brigade, 7th Armoured Division, 1942.

☐	**Sand**
■	**Dark grey**
▦	**Yellow**
▨	**Red**

brigade. The divisional marking identified to which division the brigade belonged. The divisional and arm of service signs were often combined into one 'composite' piece of insignia. Personal names were painted on by the crew in a variety of styles and whatever colours — often bordering on the exotic — could be obtained.

Most of the British M3s lived out their usefulness in Burma, where they were in plain green with large white stars painted on to hull and turret. Some received an individual number on the glacis and nearly all had white WD numbers and personal names. Some M3s were converted to Canal Defence Lights and ARVs in Europe. The CDLs carried a yellow bridging classification disc on their glacis plate with a black number 30 in it, while the triangular-shaped badge of the 79th Armoured Division and an arm of service marking were also carried. The ARVs were similarly marked. M3s converted to gun tractors in US service usually had large white stars painted on.

Canada

Canadian vehicles were marked similarly to British ones but the Canadians only used their M3s for training. Examples show overall khaki-drab with red-white-red recognition flashes with large red turret numbers outlined white. Canadian War Department numbers were painted in the usual places prefixed 'T'.

Russia

M3s saw service in Russia where they appeared mainly as delivered, red stars and numbers only occasionally being painted on for recognition. Some photos show knocked out Soviet M3s with US identification markings still legible, including the geometric company marks, which shows that a lot of Lease-Lend equipment was taken straight from the United States armoured divisions direct. One often wonders what the average Soviet soldier made of the gyro-stabiliser fitted to the guns!

Chapter Four

The Lee and Grant in action

As already stated, the M3 was a stop-gap design until the M4 Sherman became available with its 75 mm gun in a 360 degree rotating turret as originally required by ordnance; nevertheless, the stop-gap did acquit itself well in action, beginning with the British in North Africa and the United States forces in Tunisia, then turning full circle to British usage once again in the jungles and plains of Burma.

The first M3s in action were the Grants sent to the British 8th Army manning the Gazala Line in preparation for a new offensive against the Afrika Korps. Since the desert war had started the British had not possessed any 'big gun' tanks, relying on the 2 pdr (40 mm) tank gun then a standard fitting in British Cruiser and Infantry tanks. Although the 2 pdr could normally pierce the armour of its German and Italian opponents, especially the latter, it had to close to effective range, and despite the high speeds of British Cruisers, often fell prey to the highly mobile anti-tank guns moved in by the Germans. These anti-tank guns proved to be another problem to the British, who could not neutralise them with the 2 pdr, which fired only solid shot. It was left to the Royal Artillery to dislodge German anti-tank guns, if

M3 Grants being serviced by American mechanics before being sent out on tank transporter trailers to join British units in the desert.

they were quick enough deploying. Alternatively the tanks had to close to machine-gun range to spray the gunners, making good targets of themselves. The Close Support tank (British nomenclature) armed with a 3.7-inch howitzer was only available in small numbers although, firing high explosive rounds, these tanks could take on anti-tank guns at longer range, inflicting considerably more damage than the 2 pdr ever would.

Not surprisingly, in the light of these events the British were having a bad time of things and the Afrika Korps usually gained the upper hand with superior tactics, better command communication and armament from the outset. British tanks were usually not very reliable, mechanically, though the Cruisers, especially the Crusader (see No 1 in this series, *Crusader,* by John Milsom, John Sandars and Gerald Scarborough), had a high turn of speed and an ideally low silhouette but were relatively thinly armoured. The Matilda was impervious to most German and Italian anti-tank and tank guns, though the arrival of the German 8.8 cms soon toppled the slow-moving Matilda as 'Queen of the battlefield'. The German system of fighting, mixing tanks with a mobile anti-tank gun screen, was costing the British dearly. New tanks with larger armament seemed a long way off to tank crews at the 'sharp end', and although some

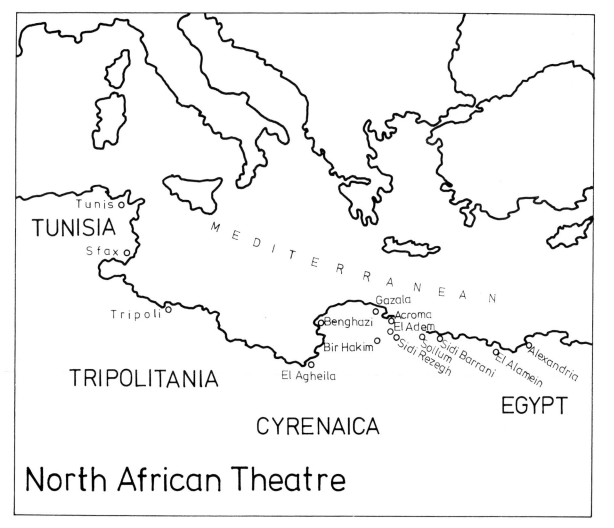

North African Theatre

Crusaders were later up-gunned with 6 pdrs it was only in small numbers at first, and there appeared to be no immediate solution. The Churchill was supposed to be 'the' tank with its thick armour and 6 pdr gun but it was only tried out in small numbers and did not fare as well as expected, or live up to the hopes placed in it; in fact it seemed more of an aspersion to the name of the great man it bore. Designs of AFVs in the United Kingdom seemed to be moving at slow pace, failure being the order of the day. Clearly something had to be done to improve the firepower of British armour. Even the American Stuarts supplied to the British in August 1941 only had 37 mm guns, roughly equal to the 2 pdr. The next tank in the ordnance pipeline from America was to change matters considerably in favour of the British.

Early in 1942 the first M3s were shipped to North Afria from the United States as part of the 'Cash and Carry' scheme to the British. About the same time, Rommel and his Panzerarmee, consisting of Italo-German forces, were re-equipping at El Agheila in Cyrenaica for another advance. These circumstances had been brought about as a result of a weakened British Royal Navy in the Mediterranean which allowed valuable war supplies to reach the Axis despite attacks by the Royal and Commonwealth Air Forces, which were also still weak from the 'Crusader' battles, and the submarine flotillas out of Malta. Even in the air the war was not going too well since the Luftwaffe had received numbers of the Bf 109F which outclassed the aged British Hurricanes and American-supplied P-40s. Clearly Rommel was to go on to the offensive once again; and on January 21 1942 he attacked across a narrow front, breaking through the British advance troops and forcing them back. The 8th Army retreated beyond Benghazi, leaving a large amount of well-stocked supply dumps to the advancing Afrika Korps and their Italian allies. Once again Rommel followed through, but outran his lines of supply; he was successfully halted by the 8th Army's stand at Gazala. This stalemate was to last for four months.

During the lull, both sides made preparations, the British digging in, improving their lines of defence and heavily mining their front, across a 40-mile stretch of desert from Gazala on the coast, to Bir Hakeim; this end of the flank was defended by the Free French under General Koenig. The British incorrectly deployed their armour behind the centre of their line, anticipating a central attack, whereas Rommel in fact directed his thrust on the southern flank.

Meanwhile, at Heliopolis and other smaller depots near Cairo, American instructors were showing British tank men their new M3 Grant tank, which would soon be supplied to armoured regiments at the front. On the Gazala front the British outnumbered the Germans in all but air power. During the temporary lull in hostilities, Rommel had received some new tanks from Tripoli; the British had received about 167 Grants from American arsenals, so the stage was set for another confrontation.

In the early part of the afternoon, on May 26 1942, the Panzerarmee made its first move against the allies waiting behind their Gazala 'line', which in reality was a series of strongpoints linked and protected by an extensive minefield. The battle, which became known to the British as the Battle of Gazala, had begun. General Cruewell's Group, consisting of the Italian 10th and 21st Corps, attacked on an approximately 20-mile front. The army, consisting of 15th and 21st Panzer Divisions, 90th Light Division, the Italian Ariete Armoured and Trieste Motor Divisions of Italian 20th Corps, under General Rommel, started their march south around Bir Hakeim at 21.00 hours, then altered direction northwards towards Acroma. Rommel's intentions — in retrospect — appear very plain, the encirclement of the allies and their so-called Gazala 'line'.

Rommel's total strength in armour was good. He had taken delivery of 19 up-gunned PzKpfw IIIs, known to the Germans as Ausfuhrung J and later to the British (after being on the receiving end of the new gun) 'Mark Three Specials'. This tank had been fitted with a 60 calibre, 5 cm KwK 39 gun and had been up-armoured with spaced armour. In addition Rommel had in his Panzer divisions 223 PzKpfw IIIs with shorter 42 calibre 5 cm guns, 40 PzKpfw IVs with 7.5 cm howitzers and 50 PzKpfw IIs with 20 mm

General Grants advance across the desert.

cannon. The Italians had an assortment of 228 M13/40s and M14/41s mainly armed with 47 mm guns. In reply the British armoured force had a total of 849 tanks allotted amongst the three armoured brigades of 30 Corps, and the two Army Tank Brigades of 13 Corps. The former had the preponderance of armour, 573 vehicles to 276 in 13 Corps which were 'Infantry Tanks', such as Matildas and Valentines. The two armoured divisions of 30 Corps, the 1st and 7th, were subordinated into three armoured brigades, the 22nd and 2nd Armoured Brigades in 1st Armoured Division and the 4th Armoured Brigade in 7th Armoured Division.

The newly arrived Grants had been allotted to 30 Corps' armoured regiments along with 149 Stuarts (M3 light) and 257 Crusaders. The Grants were allocated as two squadrons to one of Stuarts in 4th Armoured Brigade, 7th Armoured Division, and one squadron to two of Crusaders in 2nd and 22nd Armoured Brigades in the 1st Armoured Division. The greater number were placed under 7th Armoured Division's command with its solitary armoured brigade. 13 Corps' armour consisted of 166 Valentines and 110 Matildas in the 1st and 32nd Army Tank Brigades.

As with most desert battles since the arrival of the Germans in North Africa, things did not go too well for the British, and, as we shall see later, it was not quite 'plain sailing' for the Panzerarmee, although on first impression Rommel felt that Tobruk, his prime objective, was within easy reach. On the march east the Italian 'Trieste' Division navigated itself wrongly right into the British 150 Brigade Group's 'box', and was given a mauling for its pains, but this did confirm to Rommel the exact location of 150 Brigade, which he had not known existed in such force. This was later to become a problem to him. The 'Ariete' Armoured Division's objective was General Koenig's 1st Free French Brigade at Bir Hakeim, an objective which proved too tough a nut for this Italian division to crack. Whilst 'Ariete' was receiving a bloody nose from the French, Lieutenant General Nehring's DAK units swept northwards, 21st Panzer crushing the 3rd Indian Motor Brigade and Major General Vaersts' 15th Panzer's leading units meeting the British 4th Armoured Brigade west of Bir Beuid. The three regiments of the 4th Armoured Brigade were the 8th King's Royal Irish Hussars and the 3rd and 5th Royal Tank Regiments. This brigade had taken delivery of the new American Grants.

In the action that followed 15th Panzer's first contact with 3rd RTR was catastrophic to the German armour. Expecting the British tanks to deploy for close action — a common enough assumption from previous battles — the 15th Panzer Division experienced long range gunfire, blasting their vehicles into blazing wrecks from tanks of a type hitherto unknown in North Africa and firing from ranges unimagined from British armour. The Grant had arrived! And the Germans had felt its debut on the receiving end of the 75 mm gun. Unfortunately, 4th

Lee Mk I in British service in the Western Desert.

Armoured Brigade's attack did not hold up 15th Panzer, whose accompanying guns pumped 88 mm and 76.2 mm shells into the Grants, forcing them to withdraw. All anti-tank gunners did not fare so well though; here Heinz W. Schmidt, a company commander with the 2nd Reinforced Battalion, 115 Rifle Regiment, tells the story of a Grant attack on his battalion:

'A dozen tanks emerged from dead ground ahead of the companies on my right. They were of types we did not know, heavier than the tanks we had met hitherto. As we knew to our cost later, they were American General Grants, which had arrived in quantity in the Middle East, though not in the numbers that Auchinleck had hoped for. They were nearer to being a match for our Mk III and Mark IV Panzers than anything the British had sent into the Desert before. The previous tanks supplied by the Americans — the General Stuarts or 'Honeys' — were fast but not really more effectual than armoured cars. Certainly they were not fit to meet heavy Panzers.

'I held my fire, but the companies on the right let rip with the 50 mm "pak" guns. I saw some of their shells bounce harmlessly off the Grants. On the other hand the enemy's replying fire was grim. His shell-bursts among our infantry were particularly deadly. Now a shiver went through me. From out of the dip emerged rank after rank of the new tanks — a good

sixty in all. They came at us with every muzzle blazing.'*

The above action took place at the time 2nd and 22nd Armoured Brigades once again attacked 15th Panzer with their Grants around 'Knightsbridge', a 'Desert Box' about 11 miles south of Acroma. Major General Lumsden had ordered 1st Armoured Division to the 7th's assistance on May 27; 22nd Armoured had fought both Panzer divisions, losing over 25 tanks and pulling out back towards Knightsbridge. At this point in the battle the Panzers were running low on petrol, a trait which followed them wherever they fought, plus the incessant pounding they received on the march by bombers and ground-attack Hurricanes of the Desert Air Force, who easily latched on to the omni-present column of dust over the advancing vehicles. On May 28 a battle raged between both Panzer divisions, attacked on both sides by the 1st Army Tank Brigade from the west and by 2nd and 22nd Armoured Brigades from the east.

As the Italians had failed to penetrate the British minefields in the north, to open up a supply line to the Panzers, Rommel had to consolidate his position and withdrew into the 'Cauldron' or 'Hexenkessel' after finally eliminating the 150th Brigade Box on June 1. Here he stayed to await the precious petrol

*With Rommel in the Desert, by H. W. Schmidt. White Lion Publishers.

Medium Tanks M3 of the US Army advance on Tunisia.

for his Panzers, which he hoped would shortly arrive via the path that was finally cut by the Italians through the British minefields on May 31 at Trigh El Abd and Trigh Capuzzo. The time was ripe for a British counter-attack, but no full-scale counter-stroke was forthcoming so the Panzerarmee gained valuable time to replenish.

Eventually, on June 4/5, General Ritchie attacked Rommel in the Cauldron, launching the 9th and 10th Indian Brigades supported by the tanks of 22nd Armoured Brigade from the east while the 69th Brigade with armoured support from 32nd Army Tank Brigade attacked from the north. Both attacks failed, being hotly contested by the German armour and anti-tank gun screen; the British withdrew and Rommel broke out from his position in the Cauldron.

Bir Hakeim, meanwhile, still held out. The French were ordered to withdraw on June 10 after considerable attention from Special Group 288 of the Panzerarmee sent by Rommel to 'bolster' the Italian attack there. The next day units of 21st Panzer headed for Sidra Ridge while 15th Panzer and 90th Light Division ran for the airstrip at El Adem. By June 13 the British had only about 70 tanks running to oppose any threats, but the Germans trod warily

because by this time they knew only too well of the new Grant with its long-range armament and of the new longer-range tactics employed by British armour, so different from the early 'cavalry type charges' they had witnessed. June 13 General Ritchie ordered a withdrawal, the British falling back to Halfaya leaving Tobruk isolated. Rommel's ultimate goal, Tobruk, fell on June 21 1942.

On June 16 the 4th Armoured Brigade was considerably reduced in strength, only about 58 of its tanks — including the new Grants — being runners. The next day, attacked by over 100 Panzers, the 4th Armoured lost about 28 vehicles to the Germans and withdrew from the action. The Germans withdrew to Gambut. The British fought a holding action at Mersa Matruh from June 26-28 as they retreated to Alamein. The ensuing period resulted in another stalemate as found before Gazala. General Auchinleck was soon to be relieved by General Alexander, while General Ritchie's command would be taken over by General Montgomery, who arrived in the desert as a massive re-supply to the 8th Army was taking place.

In the battles up to the first Alamein the British crews found — in the Grant — a tank on which they could depend. It had mechanical reliability, good dual-purpose armament, good armour protection, and was very roomy and comfortable inside. Of course, the 8.8 cm anti-tank shells could pierce the Grant easily, but the British crews could take on the

Lee & Grant

'88' gunners with some success using HE shells. The Germans as a result were now more wary when confronted by British armour although the high silhouette of the Grant made a good target. But to the British tanker it was an 'equaliser' until the promised medium tank, the M4 Sherman, arrived in the Middle East, spurred on by President Roosevelt's personal pressure on the American Arsenals for tank supplies to Britain.

By June 28 the Germans were at Fuka, the next day the 90th Light pushed to Daba with the Italians in tow. The British 1st Armoured Division, south of Fuka, had hardly any Grants left and was ordered to a position south of Alamein to cover 10 Corps, only to be in action once again with the 7th Motor Brigade against units of the 21st Panzer and the accompanying Italian 'Littorio' Division south of Daba. Nightfall on June 30 saw 4th Armoured Brigade at Tell el Aqqaqir covering 90th Light's position at Sidi Abd el Rahman, and 22nd Armoured Brigade regrouping south of El Alamein station. The British armour fought the Panzer divisions between Fuka and El Daba in the north and at El Quseir in the south. By the next day the bulk of the 8th Army was at Alamein: 36 Grants, 60 Stuarts, 12 Valentines and eight Crusaders were all that remained in 1st Armoured Division. Rommel had 55 German and 30 Italian tanks left.

In 22nd Armoured Brigade only 18 out of a total of 28 tanks were runners, but nevertheless these attacked units from 15th Panzer, driving them back westwards, the Grant 75 mm gun again being partly responsible. The next day units of the 1st New Zealand Artillery attacked 15th Panzer's southern flanks with 30 Grants in support and gave the Germans a severe beating. Yet again the confidence the British crews were placing in their new mounts paid dividends.

Early on July 3, Rommel planned a drive to the coast by both his Panzer divisions and the 90th Light. 'Ariete' and 'Trieste' Divisions were given the task of attacking 13 Corps in the south. 'Ariete', unlucky to the end, was attacked by British tanks — with large-scale infantry support — leaving the division battered with hardly any serviceable tanks. Meanwhile 15th and 21st Panzer did not have things all their own way, being halted by repeated attacks from 1st Armoured ten miles or so east of Deir el Shein to the westerly end of Ruweisat Ridge for a cost of 17 Grants — which were now getting precious — 19 Stuarts and three Valentines. The next day 1st Armoured once again fought both Panzer divisions but was pushed back by accurate 8.8 cm gunfire. Low on ammunition, 15th Panzer had to break off action to escape. 1st Armoured Division's remaining Grants were also very low on ammunition, so both sides broke away to replenish. It would be five days before Rommel attempted another attack.

From the battles that had taken place it is obvious that the desert was littered with burnt-out and derelict tanks. Both sides operated tank recovery teams,

brave men from rear echelons who would attempt — often under harrassing enemy fire — to recover vehicles which could be made to run again, or to take serviceable parts from derelicts. This was a dicey business, as both sides tried to recover what they had lost and wherever possible each side would blow up each other's abandoned vehicles to prevent such recovery. The recovery teams either towed away any repairable tanks or put them on transporters to be fixed up and reissued to units. This way units were kept supplied with at least some form of tank, albeit not new, but if it could move and the gun worked, at this stage of the desert war, it fought! Often a broken-down tank could be towed from the battlefield by another tank in the unit, hence the long and heavy gauge tow cables carried, as well as spare sprockets — when available — track links and road wheels. The tank won the desert battles, so wherever possible they came first in priority to units. An armoured unit without tanks was as tactically useless as a gun without ammunition.

Between July 9 and 14 the Panzerarmee attacked in a series of eastward thrusts to attempt an overthrow of the British Alamein positions. On July 11, after being stopped by Australian opposition, the Germans were attacked at the western end of Ruweisat Ridge by units of both 13 and 30 Corps. On July 15 Rommel was still trying to force the Alamein line. 22nd Armoured Brigade, which had been on the eastern end of Ruweisat Ridge with 75 tanks, 31 of which were Grants, deployed to Alam Nayil but was outmanoeuvred at Alam el Dihmaniya by the DAK armour, resulting in the 4th New Zealand Brigade being overrun. More attacks by the British along Ruweisat Ridge caused losses Rommel could neither afford nor accept, so he began withdrawing because of lack of reserves. The Germans alone were 60 per cent under strength. Rommel was given two airborne units to fight as infantry to bolster his manpower. These were the German Ramcke Brigade and Italian 'Folgore' Division held back for the proposed invasion of Malta — Operation Hercules — which, of

British tank crews being briefed. Note the camouflage on the tank.

Grant ARV I towing Churchill ARV I.

course, did not materialise. Once again both sides faced each other across the Alamein line, indulging in nothing greater than patrol action, until the Australians took Tell el Eisa back from the Italian 21st Corps on July 16 and 17. Throughout August the pause continued. Auchinleck refused to attack until mid-September, by which time he estimated that he would be strong enough in armour; this hastened his replacement by Alexander.

The Battle of Alam Halfa began at 2300 hours on August 30 1942. After a series of diversionary attacks in the northern part of the Allied lines, Rommel made his characteristic southern sweep with the DAK, 'Ariete' and 'Littorio' Divisions crashing through 4th Light Armoured Brigade a few miles north of Qaret el Himeimat only to be challenged by the rest of 7th Armoured Division's mobile south screen at Samaket Gaballa. Rommel's intention was to encircle the 8th Army as he had done at Gazala, by pushing up around Alam Halfa Ridge (held by 133 Brigade). The attacks were launched by a Panzerarmee short of tanks, fuel and ammunition, against a reinforced Allied army.

The British units with Grants at Alam Halfa were in 10th and 7th Armoured Divisions. The 10th Armoured Division had three brigades under its command at this time: the 8th Armoured with three regiments, the 3rd Royal Tanks, Sherwood Rangers Yeomanry and the Staffordshire Yeomanry, with 84 tanks, 72 of which were Grants; 22nd Armoured had four regiments, the Greys, 1st and 5th Royal Tank Regiments and the 4th County of London Yeomanry, with a total of 166 tanks, 92 of which were Grants; 23rd Armoured Brigade with Valentines was held in reserve, its units being the 40th, 46th and 50th Royal Tank Regiments. The 23rd had previously been with the 24th Armoured Brigade's units within 8th Armoured Division, formed in the United Kingdom in 1940.

Since taking over from General Auchinleck, Lieutenant General Montgomery had strengthened the positions around Alam Halfa Ridge to meet the Germans with a heavily defended front. The Grants were dug-in as well as possible into 'hull down' positions, not easy with the 75 mm gun in a hull sponson, for extra cover. Their task was to use their 75 mm guns in a long-range destruction role, and to attempt to pick off Rommel's highly mobile anti-tank guns. Since Rommel was convinced that the ridge was the key to the Alamein position he intended his knockout blow to land there. The attack was fraught with confusion and delays thanks to shortages and 7th Armoured Division harrying the DAK's southern supply lines in addition to the heavy sandstorms experienced. The 21st Panzer attacked the 22nd Armoured Brigade who were under orders to hold their fire down to 1,000 yards. The 4th County of London Yeomanry opened fire, picking off the leading German vehicles, but the German gunners soon had the range and started knocking off the 'tall' Grants of the 4th CLY. The 5th Royal Tanks opened fire on 21st Panzer as support for the 4th CLY, aided by the Royal Scots Greys. The ever-present petrol shortage forced 21st Panzer to press on, trying to encircle 22nd Armoured Brigade's position as quickly as possible. On September 1 15th Panzer had fared better, thrusting between 22nd Armoured Brigade and 8th Armoured Brigade, preventing their link-up against 21st Panzer, which was assisted by 90th Light Division at this time, and by outriding units of both Panzer Divisions diverted in a southern sweep earlier.

15th Panzer attacked — without 21st Panzer's support — the 8th Armoured Brigade to the east, shooting up some Grants. 8th Armoured soon got the range, however, and shot the 15th Panzer up in turn, forcing the Germans to retreat from the fight with losses they could not afford. Besides, the Panzers were — once again — short of petrol. Other DAK units began retreating too, both the 15th and 21st Panzer pulling back under an intense field artillery barrage and constant plastering from the longer-range guns in the Grants. Rommel's northern thrust had failed. The next day, and through to September 4, the DAK was put in full retreat. Harrassed by the Royal Air Force and 7th Armoured Division, they retreated from the minefield area. Follow-up attacks by the New Zealanders were repulsed, followed by riposte actions where necessary. By September 7 the British had withdrawn within their Alamein perimeter and re-strengthened their posts. Again both sides re-grouped and settled down to yet another stalemate.

The next great desert battle was the Battle of Alamein, an encounter which sealed the fate of the Axis forces in North Africa and started their retreat into Tunisia before the final stand at the Mareth Line. The M3 Grants and Lees still comprised 50 per cent of the 8th Army's heavy tank force, despite the arrival of the Sherman M4 Medium in considerable numbers after the battle at Alam Halfa. Of the two forces facing each other at Alamein, the 8th Army far outnumbered the Panzerarmee in tanks and artillery. Another contributing factor was the wresting of air supremacy from the Luftwaffe by the Royal and Commonwealth Air Forces who bombed and strafed Axis positions virtually unopposed.

On October 23 at 2125 hours, 13 Corps artillery opened up an artillery barrage followed by 30 Corps 15 minutes later; at 2200 hours both Corps attacked the Panzerarmee, 13 Corps in the south on diversionary attacks, with 10 and 30 Corps further north between Miteirya Ridge and Tell el Eisa. The Germans had separated their armour; 21st Panzer and 'Ariete' faced the 13 Corps attack while 15th Panzer and 'Littorio' faced 10 and 30 Corps. The British armoured divisions had 1,029 tanks pitted against 489 Axis vehicles. Only 170 of these vehicles were Grants while Shermans numbered 252, the remainder being an assortment of older Crusaders, Stuarts and Valentines. The outcome of this famous battle is well known. By November 4 the Axis were in full retreat, outnumbered, outgunned and short of supplies. Rommel returned to the front from Germany on October 25, to take back his command from the 'caretaker' General Stumme, but this was to no avail. The writing was on the wall, and Panzerarmee Afrika was in full retreat fighting for survival.

Although relegated and later classified as substitute standard, the Grant continued in front-line service

M7 HMC of the US Army shelling the Gothic Line in Italy.

with the British and the Lee with both British and American forces in Tunisia. When the American Armoured Force had been 'convoyed' to England for further training and preparation in 1942, they brought with them a large preponderance of M3 Lees. In Tunisia they were still using the Lee; the United States 1st Armoured Division with its two armoured regiments, the 1st and 13th, had Shermans and Stuarts as well as the Lee. Each armoured regiment had four tank battalions: HQ, one light and two medium battalions. When United States forces

M7 HMC of the 1st French Army in action in Germany.

Above *Grant in Australian service*. **Above right** *Lee in British service in Burma.*

landed in North Africa on November 8, only the second battalion of 13th Armoured Regiment landed, with all M3s. The Shermans would arrive in the following month, December.

The first real battle the Americans found themselves in was at Kasserine Pass, a battle which cost an inexperienced US 1st Armoured Division dearly against the veterans of the DAK. At this time the 15th and 21st Panzer Divisions had been joined by another division, the 10th Panzer. The build-up to the Battle of Kasserine started on Christmas Day 1942. Kasserine lay between two mountain ranges, the Western and Eastern Dorsales. General Arnim, commander of the 5th Panzerarmee, had taken the offensive, thrusting forward to gain possession of the Eastern Dorsales, thereby gaining command of the coastal plains and the mountain passes, followed by a full-scale attack through Faid Pass on February 14 when he captured Sidi bou Zid. The Americans lost 44 tanks in this attack plus many other vehicles and guns. Attached to the German 10th Panzer Division at this time was Number 1 Company, 501st Independent Heavy Tank Battalion, with new PzKpfw VIs (better known as the Tiger I). This tank mounted an 8.8 cm gun; no Allied tank at this time in Africa had this kind of firepower. Luckily for the Allies the Tiger arrived in very limited numbers, but the PzKpfw IV with the long 7.5 cm gun was encountered in larger numbers, which more or less made up for this. Besides, the PzKpfw IV was a lot more mobile than the lumbering Tiger, where speed and manoeuvrability had been sacrificed for heavy armour.

The US 1st Armoured Division, commanded by Major General Orlando Ward, made an unsuccessful counter-attack to try to retake Sidi bou Zid, the Americans suffering heavily and losing a battalion of over 50 tanks. They fared no better the day after, losing nearly 100 tanks in addition to a large number of half-tracks and guns. The Americans were learning the hard way, but in the meanwhile the old German 'bogey man', the 8.8 cm anti-tank gun, and the new long 7.5 cm guns on the PzKpfw IV, plus the self-propelled guns (or Panzerjägers), were having what the Americans would term a 'Turkey Shoot'.

These weapons, coupled with superior tactics, were costing the Americans dearly. The M4s and M3s, both light and mediums, were taking a steady toll of Panzers and the Germans did not get off entirely unscathed in combat, but the seasoned Afrika Korps troops were very tough opposition to the virtually 'new' US force.

The United States 1st Armoured Division's regiments were in action on February 17 1943 at Sbeitla but were forced to withdraw to Kasserine. However, on February 19, after a day's lull, the 21st Panzer Division was repulsed from its attack on Sbiba; Allied numerical superiority was beginning to tell on the Germans, since all losses in United States and British armour were made up with new equipment and reserves. The M3s were now being phased out in favour of Shermans as the main Allied battle tank; and the Sherman was arriving in large numbers from United States arsenals.

By February 25 the Allies had retaken Kasserine Pass; Rommel had started a withdrawal from Kasserine and Sbiba on the 22nd. Another chapter of the M3s action history had closed, but the story was not ended. Large numbers of Grants and Lees were refitted and sent to another theatre, the Far East, where, in the hands of British and Commonwealth troops, they were used against the Japanese in Burma. A number of M3s were sent to Australia and New Zealand as training machines. The Canadians had made some M3s at Montreal Locomotive Works for their own army, but these had only been used as training machines and not in combat.

The Lees and Grants had their 'swansong' in Burma, operating in the infantry support role, a task for which they were originally designed by the United States Ordnance Board. Lees were used to 'shoot in' the infantry with their 75 mm guns using HE. They met very little opposition, since Japanese tanks were easily coped with and the M3s were proof against most Japanese anti-tank weapons. A new concept of anti-tank warfare was encountered in this campaign. Japanese infantry would leap on to the tanks with bombs or petrol to ignite, sacrificing themselves for the Emperor, or thrust their swords through turret hatches and vision slits. Crews kept revolvers and sub-machine guns to hand. Often accompanying infantry were carried on the tank hull to counteract

Lee & Grant

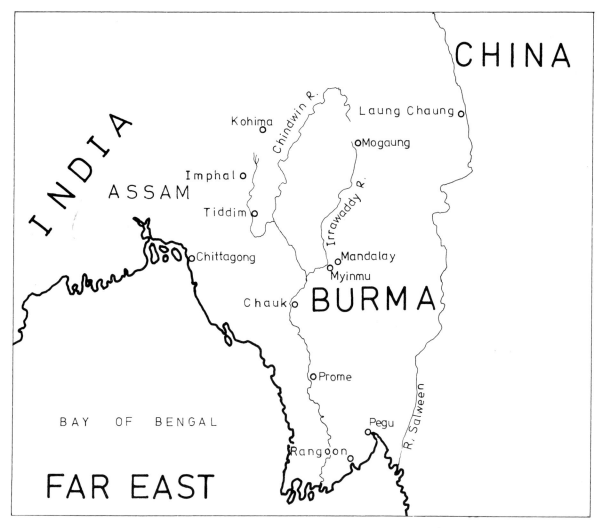

these suicide squads. This type of attack, although not unknown, was alien to the Western soldiers. Events had turned full circle once again, the infantry support tanks needed protecting, by infantry.

The Indian Armoured Corps was formed on May 1 1941. Three Indian armoured divisions had Lees and Grants, these being the 31st, 32nd and 43rd Armoured Divisions, each consisting of two tank brigades. The 31st had the 251st and 252nd Armoured Brigades with Grants and Stuarts; the 32nd had the 254th and 255th Armoured Brigades with Grants, Lees and Stuarts (the two regiments of the British 7th Armoured Brigade — which had been in the Western Desert until January 1942 — was attached to this division); while the 43rd Armoured Division had the 267th and 268th Armoured Brigades with Lees and Grants.

As stated earlier, the M3s were used piecemeal in

Lee being ferried across a river in Burma. Note that the machine-gun cupola has been removed.

The Lee and Grant in action

Top *CDL on night trials.* **Above** *Knocked-out Soviet M3 tank being inspected by German officers.*

Burma, largely as infantry support. Full-scale tank attacks on the scale of the Desert War were nigh on impossible over the plains and jungles of Burma, largely because there was little armoured opposition. The M3s did take part in many actions, units distinguishing themselves in numerous ways. The 3rd Carabiniers, Prince of Wales Dragoon Guards, along with the 14/20th King's Hussars, formed new units. Cadres of the 3rd Carabiniers formed the 25th Dragoons, and the 26th Hussars were formed from the 14/20th Hussars. These regiments, along with Royal Armoured Corps regiments formed from infantry regiments, made up (with the indigenous Indian regiments) the Indian Armoured Corps.

The 3rd Carabiniers celebrated the capture of Nungshigum as their regimental day. In this action, which took place on April 13 1944, all the officers of 'B' Squadron were killed but the M3s carried out their objective — commanded by the squadron Sergeant-Major — which was the securing of Nungshigum Ridge. Again the M3s were replaced by Shermans; the Indian Armoured Corps was constantly being reorganised, having units disbanded and others reformed; but the majority of the Lees and Grants

soldiered on to the end of the war in the Far Eastern theatre.

When the ubiquitous Sherman replaced the M3 medium in tank regiments, those M3s which were not retained as gun tanks for training purposes had their valuable and reliable chassis used for a variety of special purpose roles, from gun tractors to the unusual and very secret Canal Defence Light. The Soviets also received some M3s and M4s amongst the huge supplies of Lease-Lend material afforded them. It is well known from works published in the west the utter contempt the Russians had for the majority, if not all, Lease-Lend tanks. In retrospect, considering indigenous designs, who could blame them? But on the other hand, they only received what their allies were fighting it out in. Just as the British needed masses of tanks in North Africa, so did the Soviets in the Russian campaign. Soviet industry was under constant attack and they could not hope to produce the massive requirements of their army as the distant 'safe' arsenals of the United States could. M3s were used in action in addition to Shermans, Valentines, Matildas and even light Tetrarchs, though their roles were greatly played down or even forgotten by official Soviet historians (who also do not pay any compliments to the large numbers of Allied seamen who died in the freezing northern waters, trying to convoy war materials to Murmansk to help the Soviet war effort).

Returning to the M3's battle debut in North Africa, the British received a tank, albeit old fashioned-looking with its vertical volute suspension — that could take on Panzers and shell the German anti-tank gun accompaniment a great deal more effectively than before. The normal crew complement was six, the tank commander, driver, 75 mm gunner and loader and the 37 mm gunner and his loader. The hull sponson-mounted 75 mm gun was the only real big drawback of the tank, coupled with its height, but despite this its big gun (at the time) armament and thick armour made it well liked. There were no shortages of volunteers to fight in Grants. Another credit point liked by British tank gunners was the wheel-controlled elevation gear for both guns. On the turret gun this reduced fatigue brought about with the British shoulder-controlled guns which became heavy to manipulate when the shell case bag was full of empty cases. The turret gun on the Grant could be disengaged from the gearing to be operated freely by shoulder pad if needed as current British practice dictated.

The Grant was a roomy tank compared with contemporary British Cruisers and Infantry tanks. Three men fitted into the turret easily and even with the turret basket, the 75 mm gunner and loader could operate comfortably. The Lee saw service in the desert, though it was not as numerous as its stablemate the Grant. On Lees in British service the .30 calibre Browning was removed from its cupola and on some Lees in Burma the British removed the entire cupola and substituted split hatch covers. The

Lee & Grant

two fixed forward-firing hull guns were usually removed and their apertures blanked off, being considered of limited tactical value. Besides, there was always a shortage of machine-guns to arm other vehicles.

The British fitted their vehicles with sand shields at base workshops with racks and hull side stringers welded on which tarpaulins and personal equipment could be lashed to. Even in this roomy tank personal kit was carried outside, along with the tarpaulin sheets which made up the vehicle bivouac, or 'bivvy' for short. This was a lean-to tent, erected when in leaguer. The British soldier's natural sense of improvisation was never more taxed than in the desert campaigns. This theme and desert everyday life is well covered by John Sandars in the first of this series of Classic AFVs, *Crusader.* In action the gunner and his loader had to be a well-drilled team if any decent rate of fire and accurate shooting was required. This was not always possible, especially in North Africa where some crews were often barely trained or hastily collected teams, stiffened by regulars when occasion allowed. For some crews the only training received was in action, straight in at the deep end after hasty familiarisation with their vehicle.

Imagine the interior of an M3 in action, the vibration and noise of the engine, the incessant crackle of static and metallic-sounding commands yelled over the radio, exploding and whistling shells, the thumps of near misses or the sickening crash of hits leaving the crew members dazed and wondering if the shell had penetrated and hit anyone. Through all this the commander had to 'fight' his tank and direct his gunners; luckily he was allowed to do this virtually unhindered in British, American and German tanks, so different to the early years of the war with their two-man light tanks and the poor overworked commanders of French and some Russian tanks who had to double as gunners and loaders as well as tacticians.

On receiving the order 'action', the 75 mm gunner would traverse his gun (if it was not already there) to the 12 o'clock position and look through his periscopic sight; the loader, standing behind the gun — trying to keep his balance if the vehicle was pitching about — would rotate the breech lever to open the breech. The commander would then pass target details to the 75 mm gunner or the 37 mm gunner who layed their guns accordingly. From this the loader deciphered instructions as to the type of ammunition required, selected the round and pushed it into the chamber with his fist. The breech block closed automatically as the rim of the shell case tripped the breech mechanism. The loader then tapped the gunner's shoulder, or whichever part of the gunner he could reach, to indicate that the gun was loaded. The gunner pressed the firing button in the middle of his traversing wheel, the gun fired, recoiled and ejected the empty cartridge case. The gunner kept his sights on target to observe the fall of shot whilst the loader reloaded when the gun ran forward. If the shot was successful the commander would

Gunner's side door open showing breech of M2 75 mm gun.

order 'stop'; of course, if the type of action warranted it, and if he had another target to select, the reloading and firing cycle would continue. If action had ceased the loader would open the breech on the commander's order 'unload' and replace the round back into the ammunition rack, close the breech and report '75 (or 37) clear', whereupon the gunner activated the solenoid by pressing the firing button.

Crews were expected to perform all the tasks as laid down in the manual while under fire! Of course, extensive training — not always available in some theatres — was the answer, but as usual it fell to the gunners, loaders, and the commander as a team to decide whether the vehicle was to survive in action. Some tanks were knocked out by an enemy they did not see without having fired a shot in action.

In conclusion, the M3 mediums did what was asked of them. In action, this stopgap fared well, giving the German armour and anti-tank gunners a surprise and a headache. It helped stem the tide of the Afrika Korps' advance and it destroyed Japanese fortifications until relieved by the more versatile M4 Shermans, which rolled off the same production lines that had spewed the M3 forth into its brief career with scarcely a hitch.

PART TWO
Chapter Five
Painting and finishing your model

The Airfix kits of the M3 provide two turrets, so that either the Lee or Grant version can be built. The kits provide some spare accessories, including even a refuelling funnel, but these can be replaced by more realistic spares, such as tissue for tarpaulins and personal packs from the Airfix 8th Army figures kit. The figures from these packs make good crewmen too. If one sorts out six figures and the appropriate packs, helmets and personal kit, it will be found that the tank takes on a typical 'cluttered' prototypical appearance when all this gear is stowed around it. The figures can be modified into various poses to represent crewmen in and around the vehicle.

The kits provide all fittings so there is little the modeller can add. Even the tracks are absolutely correct. Previous attempts to mould these tracks, especially from American and Japanese manufacturers, have incorrectly placed the guide horns on each track link instead of spanning two as in the Airfix kits; a creditable point to Airfix here, as the alternative for absolute scale fans would mean scratch-building tracks up. Aerials can be better represented using stretched sprue, rather than those supplied with the kit.

Not many modellers will attempt a large conversion of this vehicle because of the excellence of moulding or its cost, but following are two easy and one difficult conversion. All that is needed are basic tools and a supply of plastic card. The M3 chassis lends itself to a lot of conversions as the real thing was converted extensively once the tank was declared obsolete. It would be impossible to include scale drawings of all variants, but this opens up a new field for the modeller, research, one of the hardest and most time-consuming factors of the hobby.

Before actually commencing with a simple conversion, a word on finishing at this time would be advisable as too many models are spoilt by poor painting or spraying with an air brush. Most modellers have their own favourite tool selection, so we will not dwell on this except to say on conversions of this scale a razor saw, hand-operated or one of the small power versions, is really necessary. The thickness of the plastic will not take a clean cut from a knife, especially on some of the interior angled pieces.

On models of this scale poor painting will stick out like a sore thumb! As on small scale models where the paint job must be neat and smooth, otherwise it looks like a ploughed field, 1:32 scale paint jobs must appear in scale. Firstly, your construction must be neat. Although we are representing armour plate, the M3 had a very neat appearance, in fact, if you look at the photographs in this book of the real tank, you will see the smooth appearance of the armour plate. Even the cast turret is very smooth, very different from the Russian armour we see, although this material was very effective despite its rough appearance.

If you use an airbrush you have little worry (though your initial construction must be accurate), but blemishes do show up and the model's surface must be very clean. The use of an airbrush really does not come within the scope of this book but if you have one you should already know how to use it on an AFV.

Hand-painters should find no difficulty with the M3's shape, except perhaps for that multi-angled suspension system which should be painted before you fix it to the hull. Build up the suspension components first and then paint them.

Make sure that your paint is the right consistency since commercial paints can be a little thick at times, and it would be wise to remember that two thin coats are better than one thick. Look at the models in displays and competitions, for these usually bear witness to time and patience taken over finish. Use a good quality brush, sable if you can afford it, and take your time. Support the model on a surface that you can revolve to get at every side with the minimum of handling. It is worth while leaving all fittings such as helmets, packs and tarpaulins off, until you have weathered the surface (if you desire a weathered finish, that is).

If you choose a desert finish, paint the basic shade of sand colour to start. After this brush some thinned-down gunmetal paint overall, letting it run into joins and angled surfaces. When this colour is thoroughly dry, paint on the final coat of sand. The gunmetal paint should show through slightly giving a good representation of painted metal. If you want to put on a disruptive camouflage of dark grey or brown, mark out your demarcation lines with a soft pencil and then paint on the second colour; it is better to paint this over the sand (as done on the real thing) in this scale, so when you come to weather the model, certain high points can be rubbed down to allow the sand to show through the darker second colour.

Next, determine where 'worn' surfaces will appear on the tank. Besides the running gear, which I'll deal with separately later, the area near the entry doors, turret and hull top hatches, and the engine cover and engine inspection doors will show scruff marks; angled edges of the armour and the areas around the gun mountings will also show wear. You can either dry brush these with gunmetal (this is where the minimum of paint is put on to a soft bristled brush and wiped off again leaving minute deposits to be dabbed on around suitable points; done sparingly it works well); or you can rub away the last coat of paint down to your earlier coat of gunmetal. This system needs care and experience so perhaps beginners would be advised to adopt the former method.

The running gear can make or mar the model. Remember that road wheels had rubber tyres and these were worn and chipped after a short time in the desert, so a little judicious modification to the perfectly symmetrical kit tyres will bring a realistic appearance — but don't overdo it! The centre axles were greased so this should be represented by semi-gloss stains in and around the wheel centres and the greasing points on the suspension units. The sprockets can be given the dry brush treatment and paint chipped off around the bolts. The teeth should be painted gunmetal and highlighted silver, but not too much of the latter. Experimentation here is the keyword. The tracks themselves were rubber-blocked and can be given slight cuts and gouges to represent wear on the pads. The guide horns should be painted dull metal with silver highlighting. Before painting, the polythene tracks should be thoroughly washed in warm soapy water. A good scrub in this should clear any surface shine away to make them accept paint more easily. You can, in fact, soak all the kit sprues in mild soapy water and shake dry before you attempt assembly, which should have removed any post-moulding solvents.

When the tank is painted overall, markings are next, if you wish to apply them. There are transfers or decals available but most serious modellers choose a finish that requires hand-painted markings. The hand-painting of markings in this scale is not difficult. Look at photographs of the real thing and you will see that many tanks had a fairly rough finish except for the WD numbers, so study your references closely. For coloured backgrounds to arm of service markings Letraset coloured sheets are ideal. These come in a wide range of colours and are self-adhesive and micro-thin. Numbers and divisional sign details can be painted on top to finish. These sheets are also good for turret squadron markings. Practice will give you a steady hand for these small markings, if you cannot buy what you want from commercial sources.

At this stage the helmets, packs and the rest of the stowage can be fixed into place. Use thin plastic card to represent haversack straps and using these straps actually 'hang' the equipment on to the vehicle, bearing in mind the attitudes adopted by hung and stowed equipment to achieve realism. In this scale lashing ropes must be shown. When you have fully stowed the 'gear' an overall spray of very thin sand paint should tone down everything just as fine desert dust overlays real vehicles, so your model will take on a used look.

Chapter Six

Detailing and converting the Airfix Lee and Grant

As mentioned in the last section, the Airfix kits come replete with stowage and various fittings, but there are a few points where the modeller can improve his model.

The Grant offers itself to various minor detail additions, notably the track guards. These were usually fitted by base workshops on arrival in the Middle East and there were a few variations in final shape. The Lees the British used were also similarly modified, and a Lee in overall sand with sandshields makes an attractive model. I've included some alternative shapes which should introduce variety. These are best cut from 10 thou plastic sheet which will appear far more 'in scale' than those supplied in the kit, which are best transferred to the spares box. If you buckle and bend these track guards, put in a few dents, but don't overdo it. Bends at the joins give a worn appearance; rivet detail can be cut from the kit sandshields with a sharp blade and affixed with Mek-pak liquid cement or similar. Alternatively, you could omit certain sections, perhaps the two front and rear portions, for a more realistic depiction of battle damage or day to day 'prangs'. When badly buckled, these

pieces would be removed by the crew to prevent fouling the tracks.

A stringer — welded on after the track guards were bolted into place on their frames — was fitted to the lower hull side. This was so the crew could stow camouflage nets, tarpaulins and their personal gear. The kit stringer has 'moulded on' equipment which can be cut away and mounted — after modification — on to a stringer cut from 60 thou sheet, which in turn is mounted on to small brackets on the hull side. If this takes a natural bend or curve so much the better as these parts soon become bent and broken in service. The 8th Army Figure kit provides helmets and packs as I've already mentioned; small ammunition boxes are easily made up from thin plastic card or suitably shaped box-section Plastruct. It is worth taking the time to lash these to the stringer, as the finished result is far more convincing than if you just stick the equipment on to the stringer. Study photographs here for ideas.

The British usually put a canvas cover over the 75 mm sponson gun mantlet to keep out the sand, dust, rain or whatever and this can easily be represented by tissue paper or the like. The gun mantlet cover was part of the tank's equipment and fitted with snap fasteners, and in the Western Desert the British made a practice of leaving this in place.

Some Grants had their glacis covered with sandbags in an attempt to increase frontal protection. In this scale if you wish to depict the bags you must make each one individually before fixing into place, not a job for the impatient.

Extra towing cables can be built by twisting thin fuse wire in a drill chuck. Determine the number of strands required for the thickness of your cable, anchor them at one end to a fixed point such as a vice, place the other loose ends in a drill chuck, operate the handle which will twist your 'cables' to the required

Side view of an unidentified Canal Defence Light heavily camouflaged with what appears to be seaweed!

The Canal Defence Light, a very simple conversion. This is an ideal first attempt for anyone who has not tried any converting because, if your efforts do not bring satisfaction, simply replace the kit turret and nothing is spoiled. Of course, this turret could be built later and substituted on a previously constructed model. The tarpaulin cover over the 75 mm gun is from tissue. The turret gun was a dummy and should be made to look as one and not detailed too much. The model is dark green with slight weathering and bears the markings of the 79th Armoured Division, but no WD numbers.

Detailing and converting the Airfix Lee and Grant   59

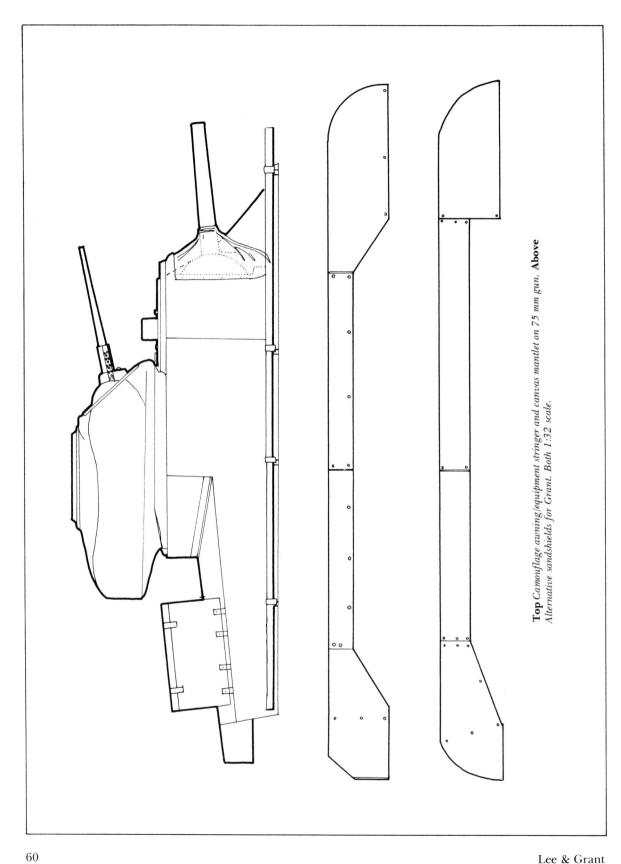

Top *Camouflage awning/equipment stringer and canvas mantlet on 75 mm gun.* **Above** *Alternative sandshields for Grant. Both 1:32 scale.*

Lee & Grant

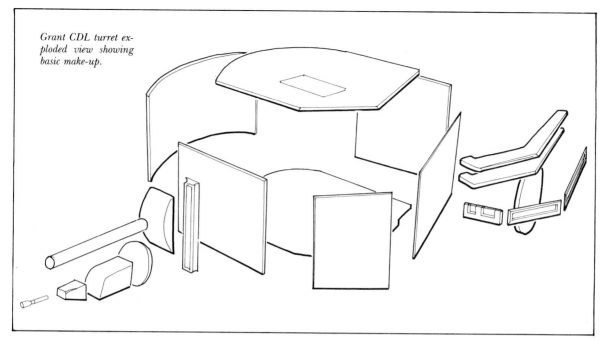

Grant CDL turret exploded view showing basic make-up.

tension. Only use a hand drill for this because an electric drill is far too fast and would give no control over the amount of twist required. You will find cables made by this method are far superior to any moulded types, and placing them on the model is simplicity itself. Ends can be fashioned from plastic scrap. When painted they are most realistic.

Some of the Lees used by the British in Burma had various modifications worth incorporating if you choose to model a Lee from this theatre. Some vehicles had their machine-gun cupolas removed and simple split flap hatches, as fitted to the Grant, were substituted. Smoke dischargers of the type more commonly seen on all early British tanks were fitted singly or in pairs on the turret side, usually the left side as they had to be reloaded from outside of the tank, possibly by the commander via his hatch.

Full-width stowage bins were fitted to the glacis on some Lees in Burma and some photographs show large amounts of coiled tow cables on the glacis, just as other photographs show Lees devoid of all stowage, in fact quite 'clean'. Spare track was deposited quite extensively around the front of these Lees.

On some Lees sent to Britain for training and evaluation the British fitted small stowage bins to the rear of the turret and smoke dischargers on the side. They also built up the hull rear stowage bins full length from the fighting compartment near to the end of the hull. Painted in khaki with recognition flashes, in this configuration the Lee becomes quite attractive as a model. Mud chutes were also fitted to these M3 Lees between the suspension units.

Vehicles in Canadian service had large cylindrical fuel tanks — which could be jettisoned from inside the vehicle — on the hull rear. The Canadians also fitted mud chutes between the suspension units as stan-

dard. M3s did not see action in Canadian service, they were only used as training machines.

Finally, not supplied in the kit of the Grant but worth adding, is a .30 calibre anti-aircraft machine-gun mounted on the cupola ring. The gun will have to be scratch-built, but alternatively you could put a Bren LMG from the 8th Army figures on the turret top, though it is debatable whether a Lakeman mount for this was ever fitted to a Grant.

Grant Canal Defence Light

The Grant Canal Defence Light makes an unusual but attractive conversion from the Airfix M3. It is very simple to build, calling for only another turret to be scratch-built to complete the transition. Any modeller, especially a beginner, can attempt this simple conversion without any fear of ruining the kit parts if initial efforts fail.

Build up the kit as per the instructions, but do not build the turret.

Using the working drawings, build up a CDL turret. Mark out on to at least 50 thou plastic card the base and top plates of the turret. Further mark out the sidewalls on 50 thou sheet, making allowances for the plastic card thicknesses when you mark out initially. After cutting out all the parts, 'dry assemble' them, testing for fit. Butting joints should have their edges chamfered for a close, neat fit. Build up the sidewalls on to the base using triangular gussets if required to support them and for extra internal bracing.

The bulge over the vision ports can be fashioned from two pieces of plastic card, spaced with plastic card strips and finished off with body putty or glass

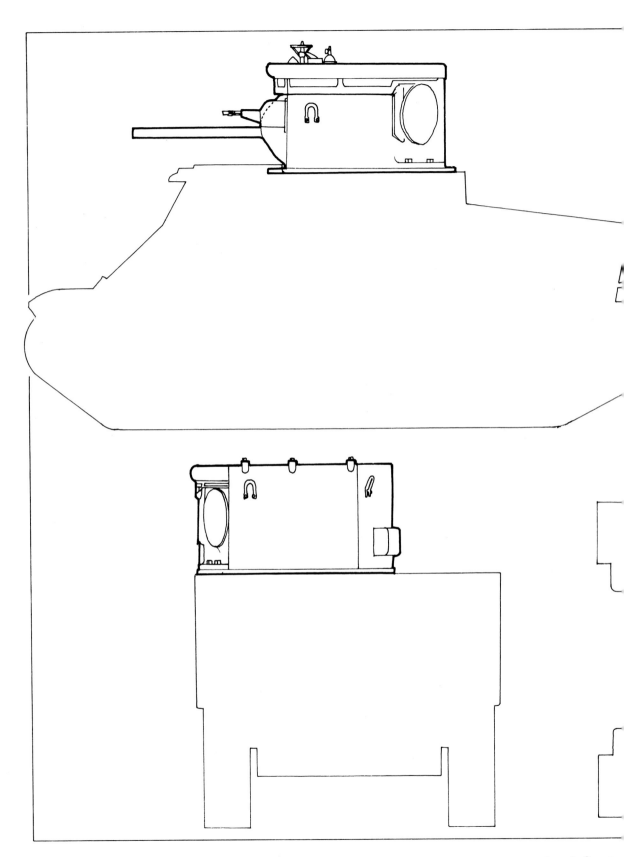

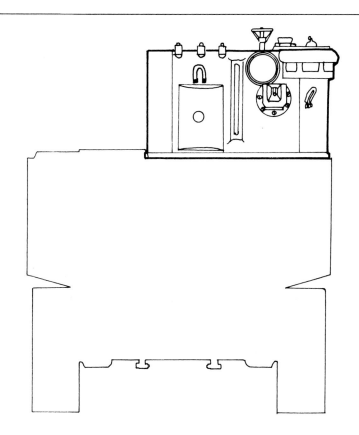

Grant CDL, 1:32 scale.

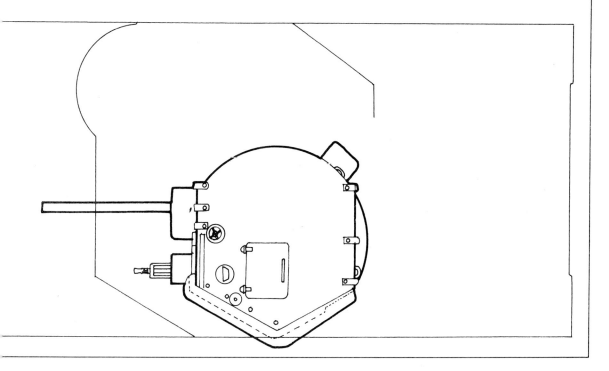

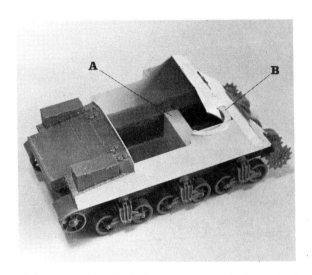

Above A *Mounting for the howitzer in place. The floor is fitted next. The undercuts have to be sawn away from the hull sides to enable this part to be fitted.* **B** *The cupola bottom former. When the cupola is in place the opening must be filled in at the bottom.*

Below *The Airfix 8th Army figures make good crewmen for the conversion to the 105 mm Howitzer carriage, the Priest. They are only very slightly modified. All the stores around the model are from the kit, from the 8th Army figure pack or made up from tissue. The .50 cal machine-gun mounting is scratch-built. The model is camouflaged sand, khaki and charcoal grey. It represents a model of the 11th RHA, 1st Armoured Division.*

fibre resin. Alternatively you could mould or laminate this part, but as it is so small a job — even in this scale — the former method described is perhaps the most suitable.

It only remains to detail the turret as per the drawings. The Besa is easily made from scrap, as is the dummy turret gun which should look like a dummy so don't drill any muzzles out. The idea of the dummy gun barrel was to conceal the function of the vehicle to distant observers and make it appear as an ordinary 'gun tank'.

CDLs served with the 79th Armoured Division and the photographs in this book show an example of a CDL from this division. It carries the triangular divisional sign, an arm of service sign and a bridging plate.

Priest 105 mm HMC

This 'conversion' really only uses the chassis, rear hull plate and engine cover plus the moulded nose plates and transmission housings from the kit. It is not difficult to make though a little care needs taking when marking out the parts.

Make up the chassis and suspension to the kit instructions. Fit the rear plate, Part 15 into place, followed by the three pieces that make up the nose, along with the brackets. You could make up a cast nose version by omitting the bolted flange plates and filling in with body putty, sanding down when dry to the contoured cast nose shape.

Lee & Grant

Cut away the rear engine cover with a razor saw where the engine grille meets the rear vertical wall of the fighting compartment and set this part to one side. Using the scale drawing, mark out the two side walls of the fighting compartment; note that they are dissimilar in shape. The left-hand side one takes a different shape to cater for the driver's compartment. Use at least 30 thou card for these, slightly over scale, but it will be a more rigid job in the end. Offer them up to the chassis and test for fit against the engine cover top and rear hull plate. Cut out a piece to slope back from the nose pieces, back into the fighting compartment as shown on the plan.

Mark out the seven pieces that form the front plate. Cut out the driver's port and use the kit driver's hinged flap to cover this. The splash guide and top hinge detail can be made from Microstrip. Check all parts for fit and then proceed to build up the side and front plates on to the kit chassis pan. File down all raised detail around the front track guards and cut away the small curved front dust guards. With the fighting compartment built up, blank off the engine compartment from the fighting compartment with a piece of plastic card. Fit out and detail the driver's compartment at this stage.

Build the anti-aircraft 'pulpit' machine-gun position from plastic card rings with a 10 thou plastic card casing: fit this to its position on the front of the side plate. If you wish to mount a .50 cal Browning build this from scrap to the drawing, but do not fit it until you have completed the model.

Above *The kit part for the driver's visor can be used on the Priest conversion and is shown at* **A.** *The gap left between the kit parts and the new conversion parts can be filled with body putty at* **B. Below** *Another view of the finished Priest model.*

Next comes the howitzer. This needs to be built up from plastic card, Plastruct and a good delve into the scrap box. The gun was mounted straight into the Priest by cutting short the trails, removing the wheels, and welding and bolting the remainder to a cross girder. An excellent photograph showing this mounting is shown elsewhere in this book. This picture alone

Detailing and converting the Airfix Lee and Grant

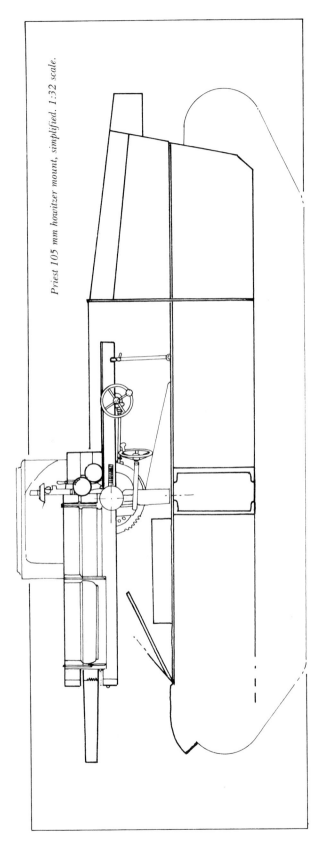

Priest 105 mm howitzer mount, simplified. 1:32 scale.

'speaks' a few hundred words. Study it carefully, then examine it closely again — it will tell you a lot.

On my model I simplified the gun mounting somewhat but you can literally go to town on this if you have a mind to. Once you have built up the gun, mount it into the fighting compartment where it is easily modified for elevation and traverse, though I fixed mine into place. Make up the recoil slide support and mount this to the rear of the slide underneath. At this stage we can fit out the fighting compartment with seats, radio and ammunition racks. The ammunition racks are built up from 10 thou plastic card. Cut the longitudinal members, mark off where the cross pieces will go and slot the longitudinal members half way and the corresponding cross members likewise, then slot them together and cement to hold. The little sketch shows this clearly. The shells are fitted into cylindrical containers —

Below *Top view of the Priest shows the engine compartment blanked off. The cupola mount is in place on the hull side, ready to be cleaned up to receive the machine-gun cupola, which should be offered up for a dry fit at this stage and cemented into place last of all.* **Bottom** *Priest under construction. The cupola has been made up ready for mounting. This is best left off until last, enabling free access to the fighting compartment for detailing.*

Above *Two more views of the model Priest.* **Foot of page** *Interior view of M7.*

these are shown in the interior shot — and stowed in these racks. The racks differed in various models.

If you make an early model Priest as used by the British in North Africa, you will need to fit sandshields. A good photo of one of these is included in two-tone camouflage with recognition flashes and artillery arm of service marks. Note the position of the WD number (S168352) and the 8th Army badge on the 'pulpit'. Also note the equipment stringers, and the large tarpaulin on the hull front.

It only remains to fit the headlamps and filler caps, and pioneer tools to the engine cover. Of course this model just cries out for a crew. Once again the Airfix 8th Army figures merit themselves as crew members.

Grant Armoured Recovery Vehicle

Another easy conversion from the M3 is the Grant ARV 1. The vehicle had its turret removed, the opening blanked off, hatches fitted, and a towing winch

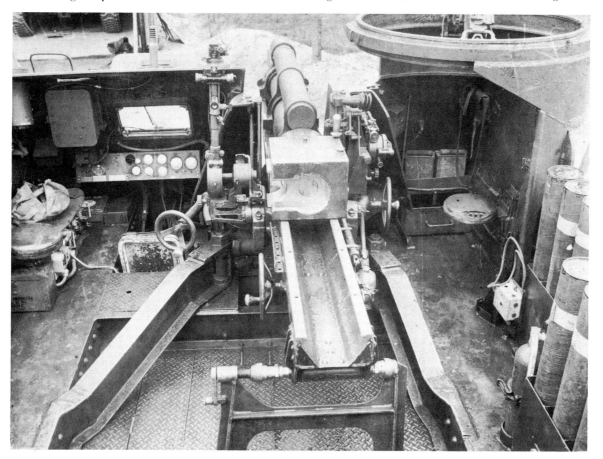

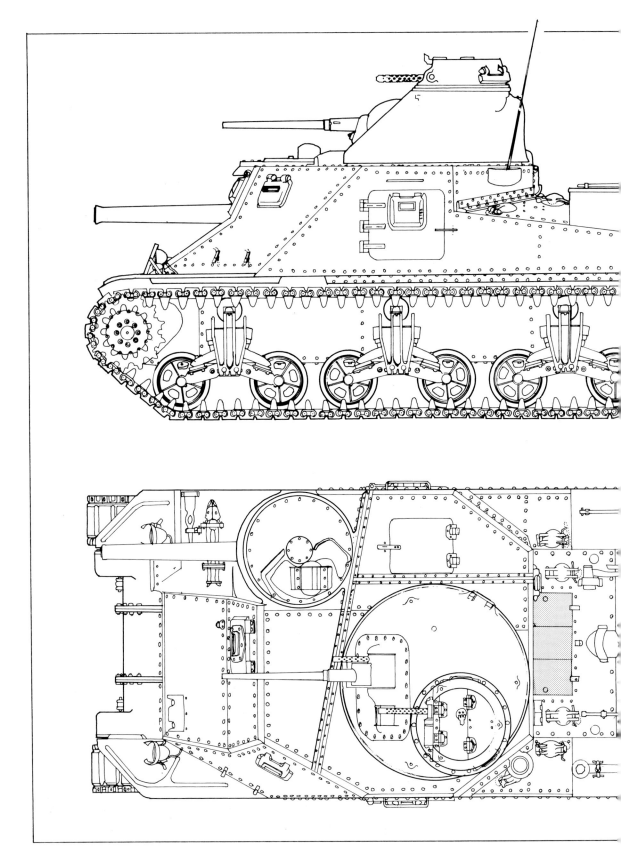

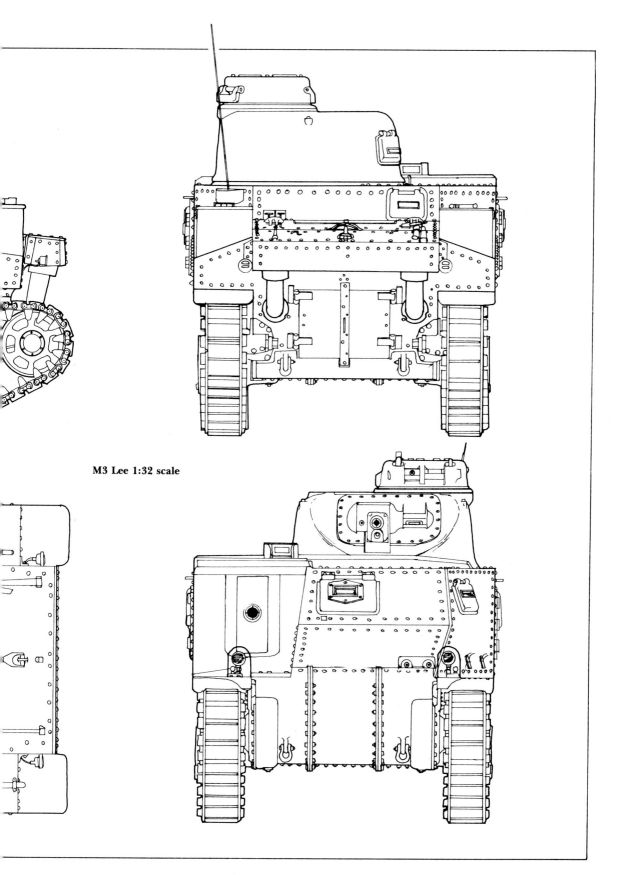

M3 Lee 1:32 scale

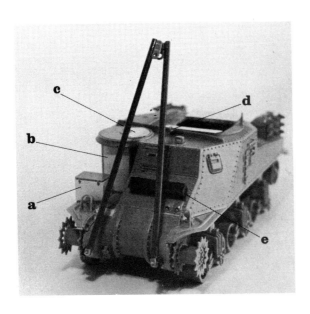

installed, For light aid recovery an 'A' frame jib could be mounted on the hull front and supported just in front of the hatchway by a wire cable stay. An endless chain hoist sheave was hooked to the top of the jib to hoist such things as engines. To recover a tank the towing winch would be used. This was mounted inside the vehicle. Some vehicles were fitted with extra stowage boxes for jacks and breakdown tools. when the jib was not in use it was disassembled and the legs were stowed either side of the hull for travelling. The pulley sheave was stowed in front of the hull sponson from which the armament had been removed.

Opposite page, top *Finished model of the ARV. The twin Brens are from the Airfix 8th Army figures box. The fine gauge chain is available from model shops. The jib stay wire is wound from thin 5 amp fuse wire. The heavy tow cable on the rear decking is made up by the same method as the stay wire, by winding in a hand drill chuck. The timber baulks are cut from thin wood. The larger two have stowage frames from Microstrip. The model is finished in dark green with slight weathering which was applied by an airbrush.* **Bottom** *The modified hull top for the ARV conversion. Note how the rear decking is kept clear to receive timber baulks and hawsers.* **a** *Split hatches to cover hatchway left by removal of the turret. Some of these ARVs had the turret left in place, but with the 37 mm gun removed, rather similar to the US ARV with its rear-mounted jib.* **b** *Pioneer tools arranged down the hull sides.*

Above *ARV under construction. The 'A' frame has been erected.* **a** *Extra stowage bin.* **b** *Sponson opening blanked off.* **c** *M1 75 mm gun sight removed and blanked off.* **d** *Jib bottom stay eye bolt.* **e** *Stowage bin across hull front. Note that the hull machine-guns are retained.* **Below** *M7 HMC, the Priest, in service with the British Army landing in Sicily.*

Lee & Grant

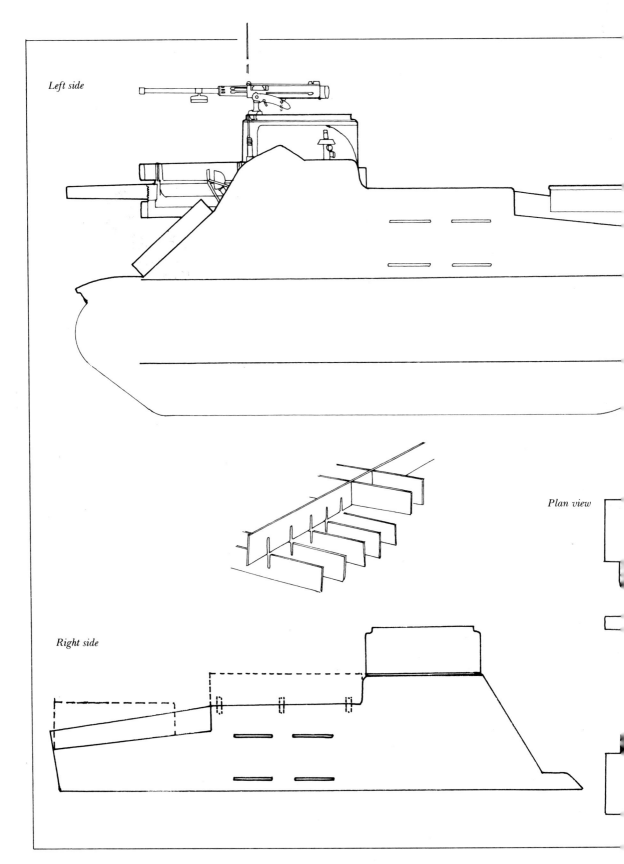

Left side

Plan view

Right side

Lee & Grant

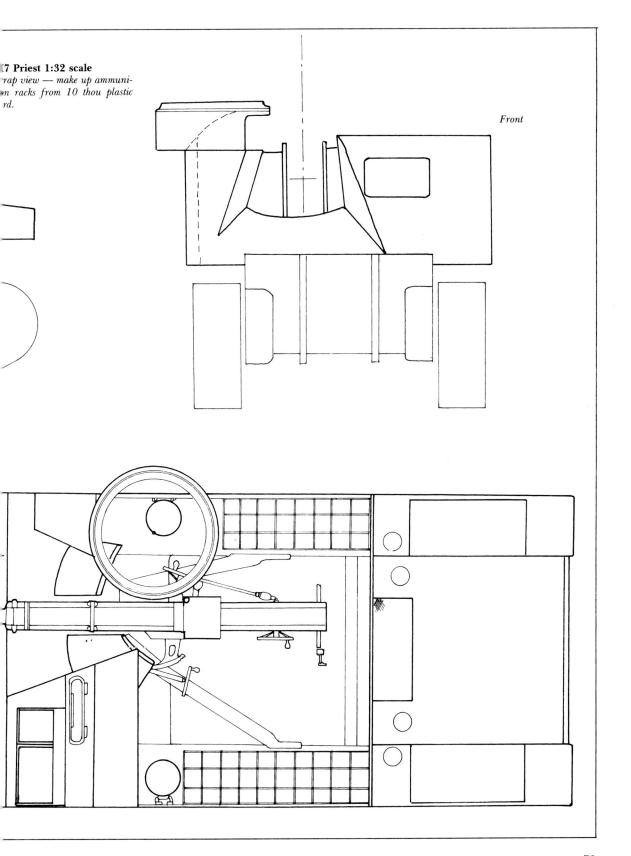

7 Priest 1:32 scale

*rap view — make up ammuni-
*n racks from 10 thou plastic
rd.

Front

Detailing and converting the Airfix Lee and Grant

This ARV makes an interesting model, especially if it is combined with another tank or vehicle in a diorama with figures in attendance. It is a very easy conversion, easier than the Canal Defence light in fact, and although there is more to do, this only amounts to adding small details and parts.

The kit is built up as per the kit instructions, though the 75 mm gun is not fitted, and the turret will not be needed, although some ARVs initially had the turret shell left in place with a dummy gun barrel fitted.

Cover the aperture of the turret location hole with a circle of plastic card, not less than 30 thou thick, after smoothing down the raised moulding on the hull top. Take your dimensions from the working drawings, enlarging the turret locating hole so as to clear the rectangular hatch opening when the disc is in place, that is if you wish to depict a vehicle with open hatches and the twin Bren AA armament in place. When stuck into place, detail the periphery of the disc with bolt heads. When you mark out the disc to cover the opening, cut out the rectangular hatch opening before removing the part from the sheet. This makes it easier to cut and hold the sheet, and reduces the likelihood of accidents to the card or fingers, especially where younger modellers are concerned.

The sponson now must be blanked off with a 'wrapper' of plastic card; 20 thou curved to fit will suffice here. Measure up the amount of card needed then — allowing a margin of a few millimetres that can be trimmed later — bend it in hot water to fit the sponson contour. When you attain the shape, bending it around a dowel of suitable diameter will help; fix it into place on the model.

Construct the attachment points from plastic scrap and cement them to the front transmission housings after drilling them. Make up the two frame sections of the jib from plastic card or Plastruct if you can get the correct size. Make the fittings — if you want to go into such small detail — as per the 'blown up' diagrams I have provided; how much detail you include here is entirely personal preference. It is possible to make a completely detachable working boom that can be assembled, disassembled and stowed.

The pulley sheave can be assembled from scrap and the contents of the scrap box should be rifled for suitable parts. Fine scale modellers' chain can be used for the endless chain hoist. A small bracket needs fixing to the splash guard that runs across the hull top. Through this bracket is passed a cable turnbuckle to take the jib stay which is a steel cable. This hooks to the top of the jib to support it.

The rear hull stowage boxes can be easily fabricated from thin plastic card, and built up *in situ* on to the hull itself. Refer to the drawings here for sizes, etc. Fit a tow hook to the rear of the vehicle under the engine inspection doors. The two drawbars carried for use with this are stowed on the left rear hull side plate. These can be made from circular section plastic

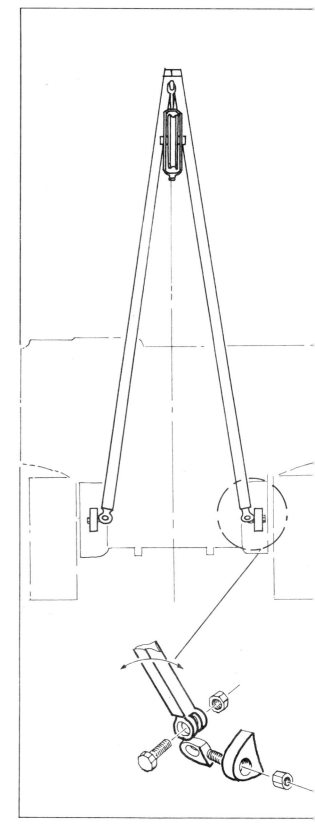

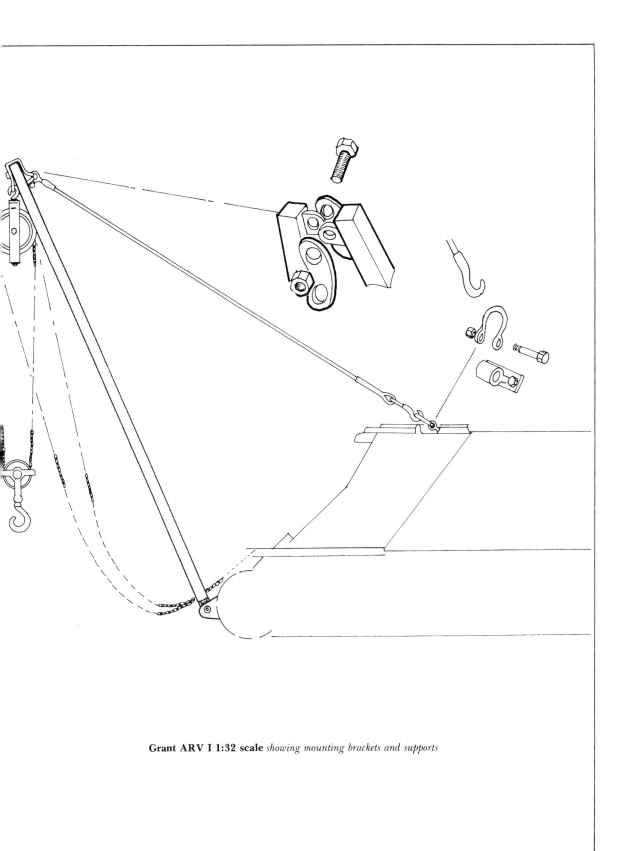

Grant ARV I 1:32 scale *showing mounting brackets and supports*

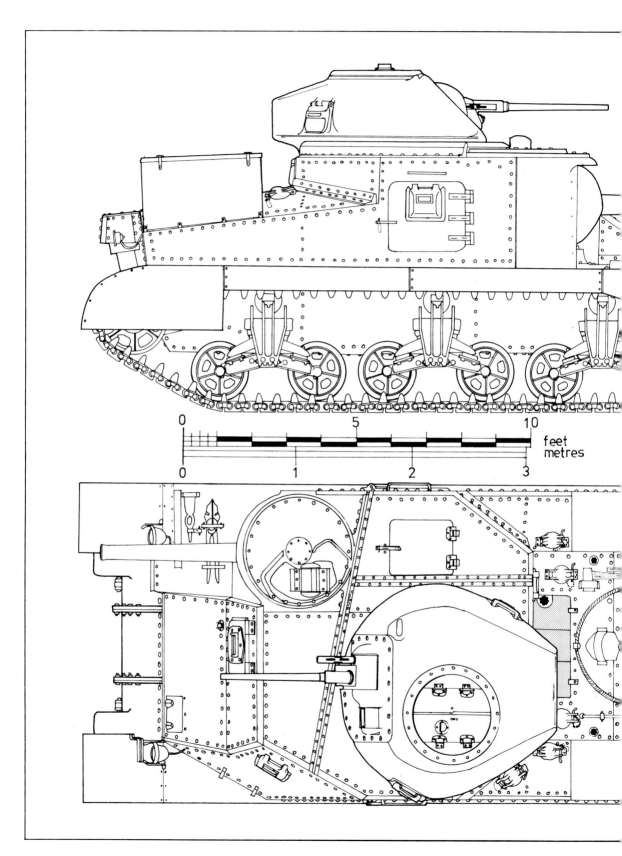

0   5   10
feet
metres
0   1   2   3

Lee & Grant

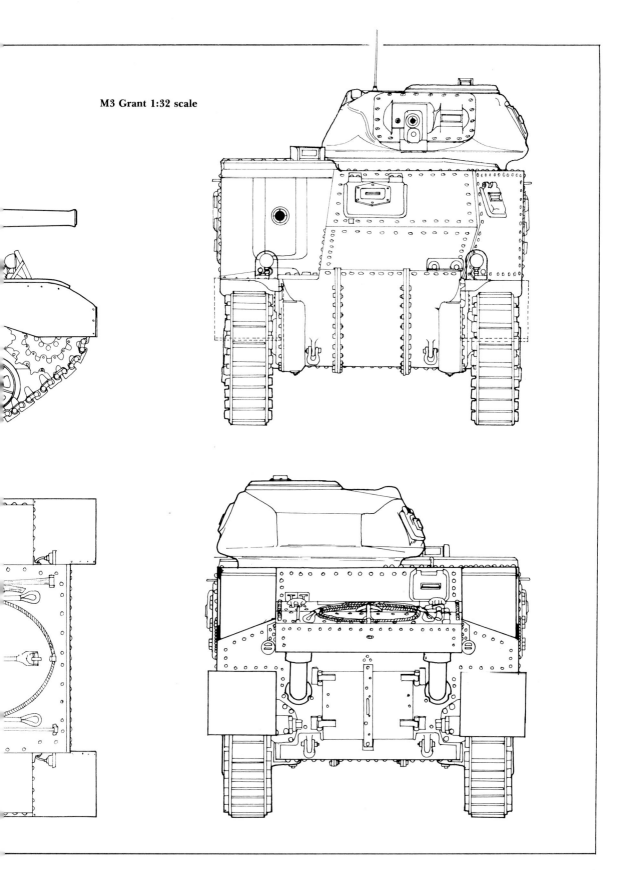

M3 Grant 1:32 scale

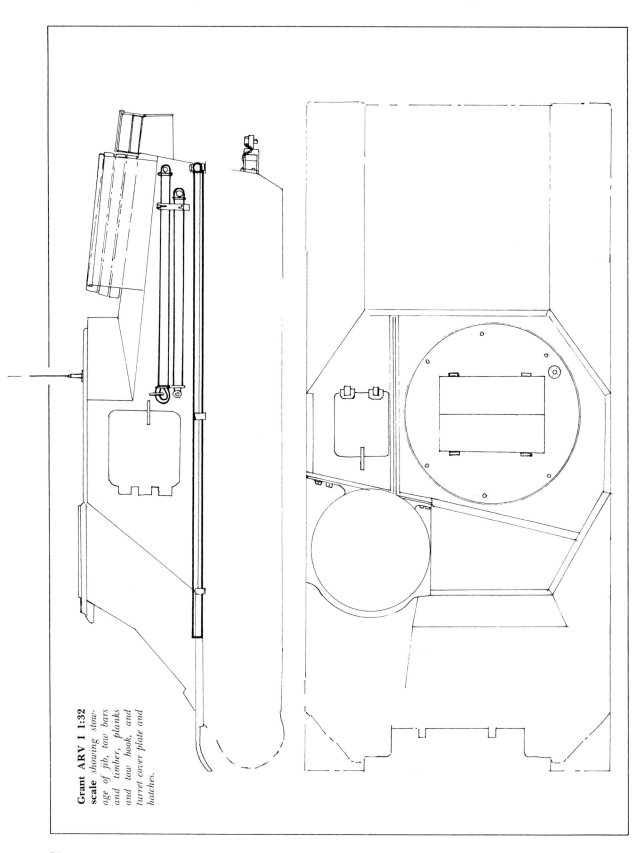

Grant ARV I 1:32 scale *showing stowage of jib, tow bars and timber, planks and tow hook, and turret cover plate and hatches.*

Two views of the author's Grant ARV model conversion.

Another view of the ARV model.

rod with the towing eyes added from scrap plastic or purpose-cut from plastic card.

Finish the vehicle in dark green and paint white WD numbers on the hull rear side plates. The side view of the ARV included in this book shows new track horns in 'bare' metal that have been fitted to the track; perhaps if this were produced in miniature it would look too 'odd', or distract from the overall effect, but it would be correct and faithfully reproduced if you did. Perhaps, again, it is that we can take in the whole of the model vehicle in one look while if

we were confronted by the real thing we probably would not receive the same effect. At least it could be a topic to open conversation if a friend asked why some track guide horns were different to the rest. Really the choice is yours, and the best of luck!

The Grant/Lee kits open a whole new field of conversions to the modeller in 1:32 scale. The chassis was used on the early Sherman tanks, and should be especially interesting to those modelling vehicles that served in North Africa. This, plus the numbers of M3s that were converted into special-purpose variants, opens up quite a new field as I've said, so all you need is the time and patience to do it.

S